RUSTIE LE
CARIBBEAI
COOKBOOK

About the Author

RUSTIE LEE was born in Hope Bay, Portland, Jamaica, and came to England at the age of four. She went to school in Birmingham, where her father opened a bakery and Caribbean food shop.

Rustie went on to study cookery and business management at the Birmingham College of Food, and worked for some years in the hotel and catering business, at one time as Head of Catering for the Lucas Group.

Meanwhile she was building a part-time career as a singer, and making such progress that she soon turned fully professional, appearing in clubs and theatres all over Britain, and touring in Europe and Africa.

In 1978 she returned to Birmingham to help run the family business, then in 1980 she opened her own Caribbean restaurant, combining her talents as chef and entertainer with immediate success.

She now has a regular cookery spot on TV-am's *Good Morning Britain* and, as well as hosting *Game for a Laugh,* makes frequent guest appearances on TV and radio shows, where her charm and exuberant humour are widely appreciated. Rustie Lee is married to an Englishman, David, and they have one son.

RUSTIE LEE'S
CARIBBEAN COOKBOOK

COLLINS

First published in 1985 by
William Collins Sons & Co Ltd
London · Glasgow · Sydney · Auckland · Toronto · Johannesburg
Copyright © in text Rustie Lee 1985
Copyright © in illustration Lennard Books 1985
Made by Lennard Books,
Mackerye End, Harpenden, Herts AL5 5DR

Editor Michael Leitch
Designed by David Pocknell's Company
Production Reynolds Clark Associates Ltd
Compiled by Marion Roberts
Photography David Jordan
Illustrated by Tony Swift and David Pocknell's Company
With thanks to Louise Bennett for permission to quote from her poems
Kitchen setting for cover photograph courtesy of Colston Domestic
Appliances Ltd and Jubilee Fitted Kitchens Ltd

ISBN 0 00 411287 3

Set in 10pt Cheltenham

Printed and bound in Spain by TONSA, San Sebastian

CONTENTS

INTRODUCTION

Well, here we are. Everyone's been asking me to do a cookery book, and I have finally got myself together and written one for you.

I hope it's going to be a book you can rely on for interesting new ideas to liven up everyday meals, or to fascinate your dinner guests - and if you've got the vicar coming, you can give him something a bit different, can't you? If he looks surprised, tell him you've been on holiday to the Caribbean. If he still looks surprised - no problem! Give him another Caribbean Cocktail Special from our recipes

Caribbean cooking is meant to be an adventure. It is bright and colourful, what with all the wonderful tropical ingredients, and it's exotic and spicy too. Nothing to frighten your taste-buds, though, because Caribbean cooking is also friendly and gentle, a blend of flavours and influences that came to us over the years from all over the world - from Spain, India, China, even Britain! The great thing is simply to sit down and savour the flavours. If you are new to our style of cooking, you will be amazed by how many fresh tastes

'Is who dat a-sey "who dat"?
Wat a piece o' libaty,
Gal yuh know is who yuh talkin' to?
Teck a good look, is ME!'
(From *Is Me*, by Louise Bennett)

in the Drinks chapter. They never argue after a couple of those!

OK, that was a joke. They do creep in from time to time. As you may be aware, I don't object to a laugh every now and then. In any case, I think it is important that this book should be fun - both on the cooking side and for all the guests who come to eat a Caribbean meal made by you.

and textures there are - just waiting for you to try them.

Long, long ago it was the Carib Indians who first made Pepper-pot, a stew which they kept simmering slowly in a large pot over a fire, and into which they threw new ingredients every day. To me, Caribbean food is like that, with more and more being added and blended in, simmering gently, getting better and better as it goes along.

Another thing. I believe that you eat first with your eyes and they, in turn, tempt your taste-buds into enjoying what you see. So make presentation a priority with the dishes you make. All those brilliant colours – especially the reds and greens – are crying out for imaginative treatment. Combine colours and textures boldly, and don't be afraid to experiment. Try unusual containers for serving your dishes in – half coconuts, pumpkins, pineapples, melons, even large sea shells. Just look around your home. You'll be surprised at what you come up with.

As for equipment, you don't need anything special, only some good heavy-duty pans – yes, even a dutchie if you have one – that you can use on the top of the stove, and a few ovenproof dishes. There are no special techniques for preparing the food, either, so that's another plus mark for Caribbean cuisine – anyone can do it!

Right. So here you are at the start of a new adventure in food. I hope it is an adventure that you will come back to for ever and a day. Enjoy it – all of it!

HOW IT ALL BEGAN

It was Christopher Columbus who brought back to Europe the first news of a chain of islands where everything was bright and green, the flowers abundant and sweet-smelling, the fruits juicy and the scent of spices was everywhere.

The ocean soon filled with traders, buccaneers and colonists from France, England, Holland, Spain and Portugal. They introduced sugar, bananas and citrus fruits and, needing labour for their huge plantations, they tried without success to enslave the local Indians. Looking elsewhere for workers, they began to ship blacks across from West Africa, and this is how the slave trade was founded.

Slavery was outlawed in the late 1850s, and many masters freed their slaves. By then the 'new' West Indians had forgotten their African languages, and so they adopted English, Spanish, French, Dutch and Portuguese, giving to each a special musical and rhythmical sound.

Next to arrive were the Chinese and East Indians, who came to the Islands to find work. They brought their own distinctive cultures to add to the mixture already there. Out of this meeting of many peoples emerged the Caribbean cuisine that we know today – a happy blend of flavours and spices from East and West.

RUSTIE'S ISLAND STEAMER

So, let's get down to it. What is so different about Caribbean food?

Without a doubt, it is a style of cooking based on the produce of the rich tropical soil. Mango, pineapple, coconut, okra, chow-chow, yam, plantain – they are just a few of the wonderful fruits and vegetables which, together with the tasty fish caught in the waters around the islands, give the food its unique flavour. In this chapter we are going to take a little voyage around the islands, seeing all the special fruits and vegetables that grow there, and I will tell you how to make the most of them in your kitchen.

Spices are important, too, and have been ever since people discovered how they could give that extra zip to the more ordinary ingredients. Every Caribbean lady has her own special range of favourite spices ready to hand, and would never dream of leaving them out of her cooking!

My own background, by the way, is Jamaica. That is where I was born and spent the early years of my life. But the food and the recipes in this book are drawn from all over the Caribbean.

As for the availability of ingredients, that should really be no problem nowadays. What was once thought exotic in Britain is now commonplace, and can be found either at your supermarket or at any Indian or Afro-Caribbean store.

One or two items, such as ackees and callaloo, are not usually available fresh, but you can get them in tins. I'll be explaining all that, with other notes on handling and preparation, as we go along.

Right now, let's set off on the first part of our journey and look at the vegetables that are special to the Caribbean. In each of the sections that follow, the plants and fruits are arranged in alphabetical order. This is so you can find them more easily when you go into action on your own. You see? We think of everything!

VEGETABLES

Ackee
Although in the kitchen we treat ackee as a vegetable, it is really a fruit and in this book you will find it in the Fruits section.

Aubergine
This is also known as Eggplant because there is a variety which produces fruit exactly the size, colour and shape of an egg. The most familiar variety is the large, tapered, deep purple one that you see in the shops and supermarkets all year round.

Look for heavy, smooth, firm fruits with shiny, unscarred skins. Except for certain purées and salads, they should not be peeled, as the skin provides flavour and holds the flesh together.

Aubergines can be sliced lengthways or crossways, or cut into small cubes, and are very versatile in hot or cold food.

Callaloo
This came originally from Africa. It is a leafy, spinachlike plant used in soups. Not usually available in Britain as a fresh vegetable, it is now appearing in tins in some supermarkets.

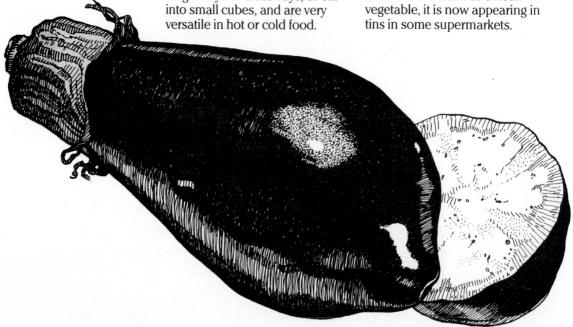

Chow-Chow

Also known as Chayote of Christophene, this is a pear-shaped member of the melon family. There are several types, ranging from the nearly smooth and oblong to the deeply-ridged and pear-shaped, and they vary in length from 13–20cm (5-8in) and from 225–450g (8oz-1lb) in weight. Colour also ranges from pale green to off-white, and the flesh tastes like a marrow.

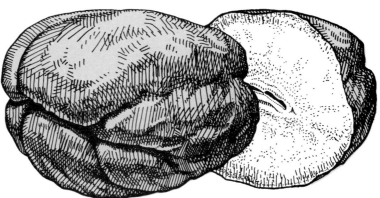

Chow-Chows should be firm and crisp when ready for use and will keep for up to a month in a refrigerator. Always avoid those that are soft, wrinkled and blemished.

They are eaten cooked and any marrow recipe can be adapted for them. They can be used either as a vegetable, stuffed with meat or fish, deep-fried, or as a sweet combined with fruit or nuts, or in pies or jams. They are more bland in taste and firmer than most marrows.

Peeled and thinly sliced, they need boiling for about 30 minutes to be tender. Remember to remove the fibrous core before serving.

Coco or Eddo

A hairy root, about the size of a large potato, which they also taste like although they are more 'starchy'. Pink or white in colour, they can be grated or boiled until tender.

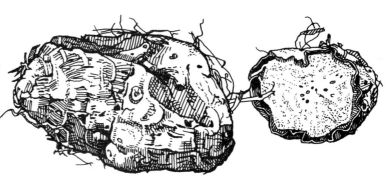

Congo, Gungoo or Gungo (Peas)

Also known as Pigeon Peas, these small yellow peas came originally from Africa. They grow on bushes rather than close to the ground, and after picking should be soaked overnight in water. They require about 35 minutes' boiling to make them tender.

Just to complicate matters, what Jamaicans call peas are known as red kidney beans in Britain. Worth remembering if you use a Jamaican shop.

Okra

A vegetable with a long history, the okra was known to have been used in the time of the Pharaohs. It was carried across to the West Indies in the eighteenth century and became one of the principal ingredients in soups because of its 'thickening' qualities. In Britain okras are also known as Ladies' Fingers.

The pods are green and tapered and are full of white seeds. Choose bright green, crisp pods that snap when you bend them. Okras will keep in the refrigerator for about 2 weeks if sealed in a plastic bag.

They are best eaten young when they are about 7.5cm–13cm (3–5in) long, but longer pods can be sliced easily. When preparing, use rubber gloves as they can cause irritation to the skin.

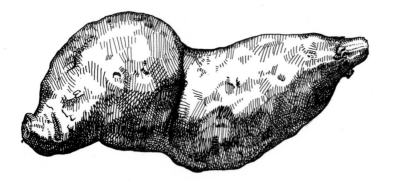

Sweet Potato

These versatile tubers are not related to the potato but are native to South America. They are globular or elongated and may be white, pink, red or purple. The flesh is white to yellow and is very tender and sweet.

They can be boiled, mashed, sliced, fried in hot oil or used in puddings.

Yam

A root vegetable which has a very tough, thick skin. The flesh may be white, yellow or, in one or two varieties, purple.

Yams are usually boiled for 25–35 minutes.

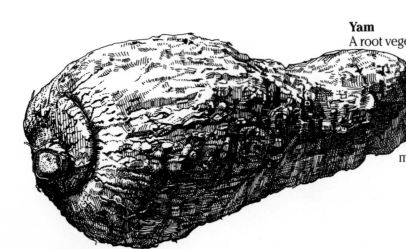

FRUITS

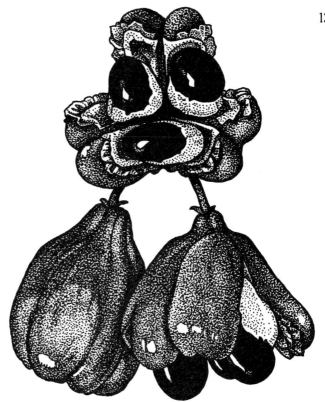

Ackee

This evergreen was introduced to the West Indies by Captain Bligh of 'Bounty' fame, and is so plentiful in Jamaica that it is often called 'free food'.

The ackee is a fruit which is treated as a vegetable. It grows to the size of a sweet red pepper and, when ripe, its hard 'woody' shell splits open to reveal 3 large black seeds surrounded by 3 segments of edible flesh. This part, if I'm not putting you off, looks like scrambled eggs. It also tastes subtle and delicious and is one of my all-time favourites.

Fresh ackees are rare in Britain, but in the West Indies they can them for export and these are readily available in Afro-Caribbean shops.

Avocado

The only connection this fruit has with a pear is its shape! Although it is now extremely popular as a starter, this has all happened since World War II. Before that, hardly any Europeans had seen, let alone tasted, an avocado, yet its history is said to go back to about 7000 BC!

The avocado ranges from small and oval to large and pear-shaped, with skin that can be smooth and shiny or leathery and wrinkled, and a colour varying from bright green to deepest purple. Always, though, the flavour remains the same.

The flesh of a ripe avocado is yellow-green with a buttery texture and a nutty flavour. At the centre is a large smooth stone which, when removed, leaves a very convenient cavity to hold fillings.

Only eat avocados when they are ripe, otherwise they are hard and tasteless. To test for ripeness hold the fruit in the palm of the hand and gently squeeze. You should feel the fruit 'give' a little all over. Ripe avocados will keep for about 4 days in the salad drawer in the refrigerator.

To prepare, using a stainless steel knife, make a cut lengthways, down to the stone, encircling the fruit. Rotate the halves slightly in opposite directions. To remove the stone, lift up with the pointed end of the

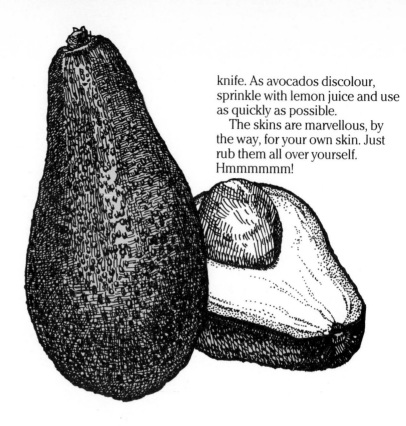

knife. As avocados discolour, sprinkle with lemon juice and use as quickly as possible.

The skins are marvellous, by the way, for your own skin. Just rub them all over yourself. Hmmmmmm!

Banana

Of course we all know what a banana looks and tastes like, but we often make the mistake of using the fruit *before* it is fully ripe.

A light sprinkling of brown speckles on the skin is the sign of ripeness to look for, and does not mean that the fruit is going bad! In fact, the more speckled the skin, the better the banana inside will taste. Always allow bananas to ripen at room temperature, never in the refrigerator, before you eat them. A sprinkling of lemon, orange or grapefruit juice will stop 'browning', after peeling and slicing.

Like avocados, bananas are marvellous for moisturizing the skin. Just mash a banana to a smooth paste with olive or almond oil. Spread the paste all over the face and neck (after washing, of course), avoiding the

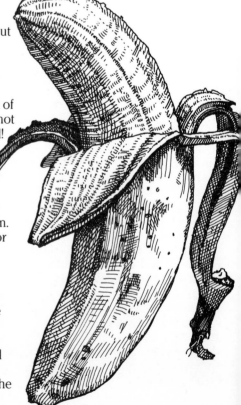

eyes. Leave on for about 20 minutes (which gives you a good excuse to lie down), then wash off with warm water.

Coconut

I have heard it said that the coconut grows best near the sound of the human voice. You think that is superstition? Well, all right, but you've got to face the fact that it has been one of our staple foods over the centuries.

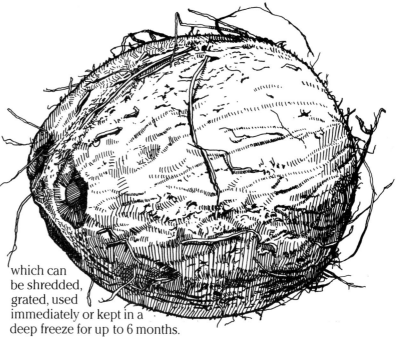

It is so versatile, too, and good from an economic point of view because every part of it can be used. When buying a coconut, pick one that is heavy in the hand, hold it to your ear and shake gently. The water inside should splash about.

To open a coconut, pierce two of its brown 'eyes' and pour out the water, stand the coconut on its 'eyes', strike with a hammer and break the shell open to expose the creamy-white 'meat', which can be shredded, grated, used immediately or kept in a deep freeze for up to 6 months.

Another body note: for a super, even, rich suntan there is nothing to beat coconut oil. Who knows, you could get to look like me!

Grapefruit

This native of the West Indies is now grown in many countries, and is available throughout the year. Always buy large, firm fruit, with fine-grained skin that is heavy for its size.

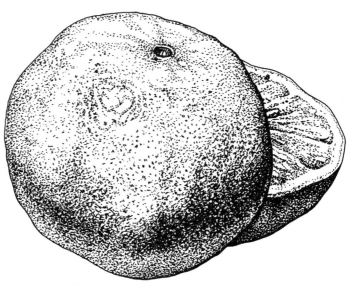

Grapefruit can be served simply cut in half, crossways, or sprinkled with sugar and grilled. The segments also give a 'lift' to salads with their bitter-sweet sharpness. Half a grapefruit provides the minimum daily Vitamin C requirement, and they freeze well, either whole, segmented or as juice. Fruit keeps for about 8 months in the freezer, and juice, 4 months.

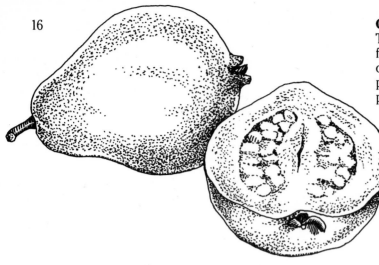

Guava

This is a small, yellow-skinned fruit, with yellower pink flesh, lots of seeds and a 'musky', penetrating odour that some people may not like.

Guavas are rich in Vitamin C and can be eaten raw, yet the soft flesh cooks and pulps easily and is best made into jelly or jam. Guava 'shells', fruits which have been de-seeded and cooked, are readily available in cans.

Lime

If you have never tasted a lime, then take my advice and get outside one as soon as you can! They may look like undernourished lemons with their tough, green skins and pulp, but the juice is out of this world. They are particularly rich in Vitamin C and also keep well.

Choose heavy fruits that are bright green in colour, but do not be put off by brown marks on the skin, as the pulp and juice will still be fresh and edible. They can be used in the same way as lemons, so, if a recipe calls for a lemon, why not try a lime instead?

The skin of the lime is an excellent astringent for a greasy skin, and when I was last in Jamaica I discovered that lime (or lemon) peel rubbed over the skin keeps the mosquitoes at bay – so you can get on with your sunbathing in peace!

1 Pepper **2** Coco or Eddo **3** Chow-Chow **4** Aubergine **5** Avocado **6** Okra **7** Ginger **8** Chilli **9** Sweet Potato **10** Pumpkin **11** Yam

Rustie's Island Steamer

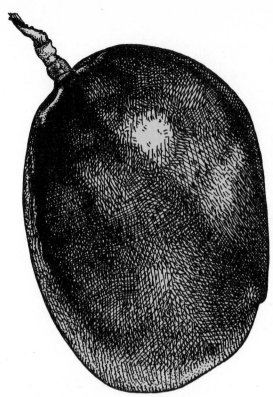

Mango

One of the best and most popular of the tropical fruits, it was introduced to the Caribbean from India, its native home. The fruits come in different shapes and sizes. Some are round, others are kidney- or pear-shaped. On average they are the size of a peach but can weigh up to 1.4kg (3lb). They have tough, hard skins which range in colour from green to yellow, orange or red, and the flesh is orange-yellow with a delicate fragrance and a slightly 'spicy' taste.

If you intend to use the fruit immediately, choose mangoes that are softer to the touch and yellowish-red, but if you wish to ripen the fruit at home, then choose those that are firm and slightly green and wrap them in paper. Fully ripe fruit can be stored in the refrigerator.

Ortanique

A cross between an orange and a tangerine, it has orange-yellow skin and a sweet, juicy orange-coloured flesh. It can be used as a dessert fruit or in marmalade as a substitute for oranges.

To prepare, remove the peel in one continuous strip, if you can, and take all the white pith with you. Remove each segment from its surrounding membrane and hold the fruit over a bowl to collect the juice.

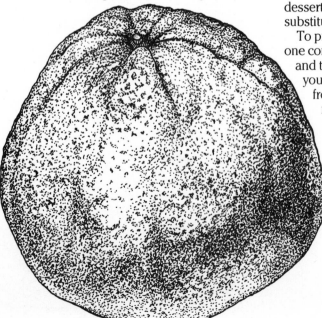

Paw-Paw or Papaya

Sometimes known as the Tree Melon, paw-paws were known to have been cultivated by the Aztecs and the Mayas. From the outside, it looks like a green hand-grenade and not particularly inviting, but cut one open and, hey presto! beautiful golden or coral-coloured flesh is revealed, and a centre full of tiny, black shiny seeds, which should be scraped out with a spoon as they taste rather 'peppery'.

A ripe paw-paw should 'give' when squeezed gently between the palms of the hands, but if the fruit you have is still too hard, then leave it in the airing cupboard or in a paper bag in a warm place; it will soon soften.

The leaves and the flesh contain a natural meat tenderizer – papain – and they are used for this purpose in the West Indies.

Pineapple

For centuries it was a symbol of luxury, and only monarchs and the nobility could taste the flavour of this superb fruit. Now, thank goodness, we can all buy pineapples, fresh or canned!

A ripe, fresh pineapple, with its spiky leaf crown, will be fragrant and juicy and will 'give' slightly under pressure. It should also be free of blemishes. When cut open, a long 'woody' core can be seen running lengthways through the centre, and you should remove this because it is inedible. Serve either halved or quartered, or peeled and cut in pieces.

A pineapple makes an excellent way to end a rich meal, because it contains an enzyme, bromeline, which aids digestion. This only works if you can eat the fruit raw, as the enzyme is destroyed by cooking.

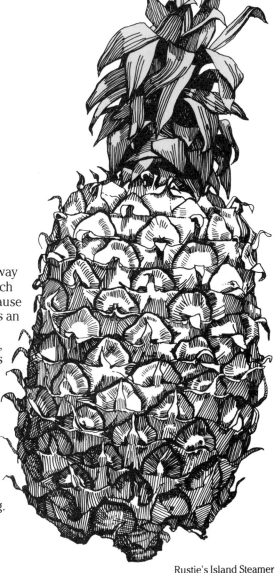

Rustie's Island Steamer

Plantain

This member of the banana family is only eaten cooked. It is high in food value, and easily digested. Plantains resemble bananas but are generally larger and are sold individually rather than in bunches. They have 3 or 4 clearly defined sides and the skin is tougher.

You can either buy them at the green stage and allow them to ripen at room temperature, or buy them fully ripe as you would bananas. (Wrapping in paper will retard the ripening process.)

Green plantains are used quite a lot in Caribbean cooking and require special handling, since the thick skin clings tightly to the fruit and tends to break off in little pieces. To peel one properly, you take a sharp knife, slice off the ends and cut the plantain in half. Make 4 evenly spaced, lengthways slits in the skin of each half, cutting through the flesh from one end to the other. Then, starting at the corner edge of one slit, lift the skin away a strip at a time, pulling it off crossways rather than along the length of the fruit.

Plantains go well in soups, stews and as a dessert – and you can cook them any way you choose. Bake them, roast them in their skins, boil, sautée or deep-fry them. They love it whatever you do!

Ugli

Sometimes called a Tangelo, but looking more like a lumpy grapefruit, the ugli is far from beautiful to look at. However, this very strange fruit, called Hoogly in Jamaica, in fact tastes absolutely delicious – a cross between a tangerine and a grapefruit, but sweeter, with yellow-pink flesh that is very juicy and has few pips.

The season is a short one, from October to February, and the ugli is often in short supply, but it is well worth tracking down. It can be used as an alternative in any recipe that specifies oranges. Uglis freeze well and can be kept for up to 3 months.

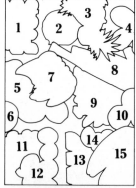

1 Guava 2 Melon 3 Pineapple
4 Paw-Paw 5 Coconut 6 Green
Coconut 7 Banana 8 Sugar Cane
9 Prickly Pear 10 Grapefruit
11 Lime 12 Mango 13 Avocado
14 Kidney Mango 15 Plantain

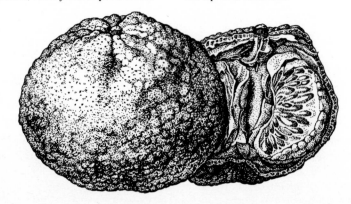

Rustie's Island Steamer

Watermelon

Whenever I see a great slice of this pink-fleshed fruit, I think of a great big happy grin. And what a refreshing thing that is!

Watermelon is a natural refresher, being about 90 per cent water in spite of those seeds which, by the way, are considered a great delicacy in some countries, and which also yield cooking oil. A ripe watermelon should sound dull and flat when you thump it, and the skin should be dark green and glistening.

It is a marvellous aid to slimming, being so low in calories and high in vitamins and minerals, especially potassium.

SPICES

Chilli

Chillies add a marvellous pungency to Caribbean cookery and are a staple ingredient of many dishes. The plant is a member of the Capsicum family, and the pod ranges from red to orange and yellow, varying greatly in intensity of its flavour. A good rule is: the smaller, darker and more pointed the pepper, the hotter it will be.

Chillies can be used fresh or as chilli powder. If used fresh, be sure to handle them with great care. They contain powerful oils which may burn the skin and cause irritation to the eyes, so wear rubber gloves to handle them, avoid touching the face, and remember that a little goes a long way!

To prepare, rinse the chillies clean under cold running water and pull out the stalks. Cut the pods in half, brush out the seeds with the fingers and remove the pith inside with a sharp knife. The chillies may be used at once or soaked in cold salted water for about $1\frac{1}{2}$ hours to make them less 'hot'.

Cinnamon

This grows on a tree which is a member of the Laurel family, and has been a much-valued spice since ancient times. It comes from the dried inner bark of the tree, which curls up into a quill as it dries, and it has a sweet, musky flavour.

If you can, buy cinnamon in 'shavings', as it is of better quality and keeps better. It can also be purchased as sticks. These are used in mulled wine and punch, and in pickling. Ground cinnamon is used for baking cakes and biscuits and sprinkled on the tops of puddings and custards.

Cinnamon is a stimulant, an aid

to digestion, and will soothe gastric upsets. It loses its aroma quickly, and should be stored in screw-top glass jars.

Ginger

Cultivated since earliest times, ginger is considered in some parts of the world to be an essential part of the diet as a guard against disease and as an aid to digestion. The West Indies are reputed to grow the best ginger and the knobbly roots are used fresh, dried, ground or preserved

If using fresh, always peel the root then grate. The root can be kept moist by burying it in the garden, in a pot. Ginger can be used in cakes, puddings, biscuits, soups or with meat. It is a strong stimulant and can be helpful when you have a cold.

Mace

In earlier times, mace was one of the most expensive of spices and was greatly valued. It is the aromatic, lacy outer covering of the nutmeg, but smells and tastes much stronger. It is sold whole, as 'blade' mace, or is ground, and should always be stored in screw-top glass jars.

Mace can be substituted for nutmeg in most recipes for sweets and can be used as a seasoning for vegetables and meats. Ground mace, added sparingly to chocolate or cocoa being used for cakes or desserts, will give a little boost to the flavour.

Nutmeg

This is the dark brown nut or 'stone' which is inside the mace covering (see above). During commercial production, it is often whitened with lime to preserve against attack from worms. Sold whole or ground, its scent diminishes quickly when exposed to the air, so it must be stored in a screw-top jar. Nutmeg can be used with most foods, sweet or savoury, and as a seasoning for mulled wine, hot milk or chocolate. It prevents that 'drowsy' feeling after a big midday meal, and is good for the circulation and digestion.

Pimento

Also known as Allspice or Jamaica Pepper, it was first brought to Europe by Columbus from Jamaica, its true country of origin, and was known to have been used by the Aztecs to flavour their drinks.

Called Allspice because its berries smell like a blend of cinnamon, cloves and nutmeg, it is used whole for marinades, pickles and chutneys, and ground for cakes and puddings. It is also used in a favourite West Indian drink: Pimento Dram.

Saffron

This is the world's most expensive spice. It is derived from the crocus, and in olden times was used for its medicinal purposes and as a dye. It produces a full range of yellow and orange shades for food, giving a beautiful colour to rice, and has a spicy, slightly bitter taste. Sold whole, the thread-like strands, which are the dried flower stigmas, are packed into sachets. To use, these threads should be crushed, then soaked in hot liquid, thus forming the 'stock' part of the dish. It should be stored away from the light in screw-top jars, and, remember, a little goes a long way!

SOUPS AND SAUCES

FISH SOUP
Serves 6

Here is a delicious fish soup. The 'spinners' that go with it are a kind of thickening agent which you roll out long between your fingers so they look a bit like thin sausages.

For 'spinners' to put in soup
50g (2oz) plain flour
50g (2oz) cornmeal
water to bind
pinch of salt

METHOD 1 Boil up 575ml (1pt) water. Prepare the spinners by mixing the flour, cornmeal and salt together with the water to make a dough.
2 Roll into strips using your hands, and drop into boiling water. Cook for 10 minutes.
3 Chop onion and pepper, and mash tomato to a pulp. Add to water together with tomato purée, seasoning and herbs.
4 Simmer for 10 minutes. Cover with a tight lid.
5 Chop fish and dissolve 2 dsp of cornflour in a small amount of water, to thicken soup.
6 Add fish, cornflour and white wine to the pan and simmer gently for 10 minutes, stirring occasionally.
7 Add shrimps and simmer for a further 5 minutes.
8 Pour into a tureen and garnish with remaining shrimps and parsley.

575ml (1pt) water
1 large onion
1 medium green pepper, de-seeded and chopped
1 large can of tomatoes or 1.4kg (3lb) fresh, peeled tomatoes
50g (2oz) tomato purée
1 tsp basil
2 tsp salt
1 tsp pepper
450g (1lb) firm white fish (your choice)
2 dsp cornflour
425ml (¾pt) dry white wine
110g (4oz) shrimps (save half for decoration)
parsley for garnish

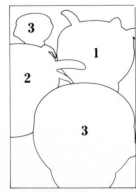
1 Fish Soup **2** Callaloo Soup
3 Pepper-Pot Soup

'When crab walk too much, him
lose him claw.'

CALLALOO SOUP
Serves 4

This traditional soup developed
over the years and is now
considered by many to be the
'King of Soups'. Its dark green
colour is very different and its
taste is out of this world!

110g (4oz) salt pork or 6 slices of
    lean bacon
450g (1lb) callaloo leaves, or
    spinach or chinese cabbage
1 small onion, chopped
$\frac{1}{4}$ tsp thyme
1.4 l ($2\frac{1}{2}$pt) chicken stock
225g (8oz) crabmeat, flaked
8 crab claws
1 tbsp butter
salt and pepper
1 small green sweet pepper, sliced

For the cornmeal 'spinners'
110g (4oz) cornmeal
110g (4oz) plain flour
$\frac{1}{2}$ tsp salt
water to bind

METHOD 1 Cut the pork or
bacon into 1.2cm ($\frac{1}{2}$in)
pieces. Chop the greens roughly.
2 Put in a saucepan or cooking
pot, together with the onions,
thyme and chicken stock. Cook
for about 20 minutes until the
meat is tender.
3 Mix the spinner ingredients to a
dough.
4 Roll strips of the dough
between the fingers and drop
these into the soup.
5 Add the flaked crab and claws
and cook for a further 15 minutes
until tender.
6 Stir in the butter and season to
taste. Garnish with the green
pepper slices.
See illustration on page 25

PEPPER-POT SOUP
Serves 4

This dish was originated by the
Carib Indians. Their soup was
cooked in a huge pot over a fire
and was kept going for weeks and
months by adding new
ingredients daily.
    Pepper-pot is said to be
enhanced with age, but it is so
tasty, I doubt you will be able to
keep it that long! Serve it as a
main course.

450 g (1lb) shin of beef
450g (1lb) red kidney beans or
    2 cans of beans
5 leaves of spinach
2 medium onions
2 medium tomatoes, peeled
1 tsp salt
1 tsp black pepper
1 dsp thyme
1 clove garlic
1 beef stock cube
450g (1lb) yam or potatoes
225g (8oz) pumpkin
1 chilli pepper (or 2 if you are
    brave!)
1.8 l (3pt) water

For dumplings to put in soup
350g (12oz) plain flour
110g (4oz) cornmeal
$\frac{1}{2}$ tsp salt
water to bind

METHOD 1 Wash and cut
meat. Cover with water
and boil with the beans for 15–20
minutes.
2 Chop vegetables and add to
pan with other ingredients. Cook
for 1 hour.
3 To make dumplings mix flour,
cornmeal and salt with a little
water. Roll into balls with your
hands.
4 Drop into the boiling mixture
and cook for the final 15 minutes.
See illustration on page 25

POTATO SOUP CREOLE
Serves 4

A most economical yet nourishing soup, so easy to make for those cold winter days!

350g (12oz) sweet potatoes
1.1l (2pt) water
1 tbsp lard
2 small onions, chopped
110g (4oz) celery
1 tbsp (heaped) plain flour
salt and pepper to taste
110ml (4 fl oz) fresh single cream
parsley for garnish

METHOD 1 Boil the sweet potatoes in 1.1l (2pt) water and mash them. Keep the water. Melt the lard in a pan, add the onions and celery and cook for 10 minutes, stirring all the time.
2 Add 275ml ($\frac{1}{2}$pt) of the potato water, and the flour. Bring to the boil, and boil for 10 minutes.
3 Add the mashed potatoes, salt and pepper and 850ml (1$\frac{1}{2}$pt) water.
4 Cook the soup for 1 hour, simmering gently.
5 Before serving, stir in the cream and garnish with parsley.

GUNGO PEA SOUP
Serves 6

450g (1lb) pumpkin, cubed
450g (1lb) gungo peas
1.8l (3pt) chicken stock
2 small onions, finely chopped
1 clove garlic, crushed
1 chilli pepper, chopped or 1 tsp chilli powder
salt and pepper
chopped parsley for garnish

METHOD 1 Peel and cut the pumpkin into 1.2cm ($\frac{1}{2}$in) cubes.

2 With the exception of the salt, pepper and parsley, combine all the other ingredients in a large pan.
3 Cover and simmer until the peas are tender and the pumpkin begins to disintegrate and thicken the soup (about 40–45 minutes).
4 Season and garnish with the parsley.

GRAPEFRUIT LICK-ME-BACK
Serves 4

No it's not rude – just so delicious you want to 'lick it back', as they say in the Caribbean. 'Knock it back' is maybe the nearest way of putting it in English English.

425ml ($\frac{3}{4}$pt) strained grapefruit juice
3 tbsp strained orange juice
3 tbsp lemon juice
dash of rum
2 or 3 grapefruit (according to size)
150ml ($\frac{1}{4}$pt) boiling water
1 pkt lemon jelly
75g (3oz) brown sugar
sprigs of mint

METHOD 1 Blend the juices and the rum in a jug.
2 Peel the grapefruit and divide into segments. Remove the pith and pips. Chop.
3 Dissolve the jelly, add the sugar and stir well. Leave to cool.
4 Stir in the chopped segments, and add the juices and rum. Pour into individual dishes and chill thoroughly.
5 Garnish with mint before serving.

**'Angelina a go plant de gunga
Bring me half a hoe.'**
(Traditional song)

WEST INDIAN SAUCE
Serves 4

More of a meal than a sauce!
Serve very hot with rice, eggs or
fish.

450g (1lb) shrimps or prawns
strained juice of 2 lemons
175g (6oz) butter
2 medium tomatoes, skinned and
    finely chopped
2 small onions, finely chopped
3 cloves garlic, chopped
bunch of parsley, chopped
$\frac{1}{4}$ tsp black pepper
2 tsp salt
275ml ($\frac{1}{2}$pt) fish stock
2 eggs
2 tbsp vinegar

METHOD 1 Soak the shrimps
or prawns in the lemon
juice for about 10 minutes.
2 Heat the butter and fry the
tomatoes, onions, garlic, parsley
until a golden colour. Season with
pepper and salt.
3 Continue frying till all the butter
has been absorbed.
4 Pour on the fish stock, stirring
continuously.
5 Drain the shrimps or prawns
and add to the sauce. Cook for a
further 10 minutes, over a low
heat, until the fish is soft.
6 Remove from the heat. Beat the
eggs, blend slowly with the
vinegar and stir into the sauce
just before serving.

Note Never allow this sauce to
boil.

SPICY TOMATO SAUCE
Serves 4

This is a delicious and versatile
sauce that you can add to all
kinds of dishes – even non-
Caribbean ones such as
spaghetti.

110g (4oz) salt pork
1 dsp vegetable oil
175g (6oz) onions, finely
    chopped
3 cloves garlic, finely chopped
2 medium-sized peppers, seeds
    and pith removed, finely
    chopped
115g (4oz) lean ham, cut into
    1.2cm ($\frac{1}{2}$in) dice
700g (1$\frac{1}{2}$lb) large tomatoes,
    peeled, seeded and
    chopped
2 tsp coriander
1 tsp oregano
1 tsp salt
fresh ground black pepper

METHOD 1 Fry the salt pork in
a large, heavy pan until
golden grown.
2 Discard pork using a perforated
spoon. Heat the remaining fat in
the pan.
3 Drop in the onions, garlic and
peppers. Cook for 5–10 minutes
over a moderate heat, stirring
continuously, until soft but not
brown.
4 Add diced ham, chopped
tomatoes, coriander, oregano,
salt and pepper.
5 On a low heat, cover the pan
tightly and simmer for 30–35
minutes, stirring occasionally.
6 Pour the sauce into a large
container. Allow to cool. Covered
tightly and stored in the
refrigerator, this sauce can be
kept for up to 2 weeks.

HUNTER'S SAUCE
Serves 6

This is a tangy sauce which is really good with game birds or turkey.

25g (1oz) plain flour
25g (1oz) butter
150ml ($\frac{1}{4}$pt) orange juice
150ml ($\frac{1}{4}$pt) water
salt and pepper
1 tsp cayenne pepper
rind and juice of 1 orange
1$\frac{1}{2}$ tbsp redcurrant jelly
2 tbsp rum

 1 Mix the flour and the butter to a smooth paste.
2 Mix the orange juice and water together in a jug. Pour a small amount into a saucepan. Drop little balls of the flour/butter mixture into the saucepan, and, stirring all the time, continue until all the mixture and the liquids are used up.
3 Season with salt and pepper. Add the cayenne pepper and the grated rind.
4 Stirring continuously, simmer over a low heat for 5 minutes.
5 Add the redcurrant jelly and cook until it melts.
6 Just before serving, add the rum.

BARBECUE SAUCE FOR STEAK
Serves 8-10

It's got a lot of ingredients, but put them all together and you will find this a great sauce for steaks and spareribs. Refrigerated, it will keep for a week.

150ml ($\frac{1}{4}$pt) vegetable oil
3 tbsp vinegar
scant 275ml ($\frac{1}{2}$pt) boiling water
2 tbsp Worcestershire sauce
2 small onions, chopped
2 chillies, de-seeded and finely chopped, or 2 tsp chilli powder
2 cloves garlic, grated
1 tbsp brown sugar
2 tsp French mustard
1 tsp salt
1 tsp paprika
1 tsp thyme
1 tsp sage
bunch of parsley, finely chopped
bunch of chives, chopped
dash of Tabasco sauce

METHOD 1 Put all ingredients into a saucepan and mix well.
2 Cook over a low heat for 15 minutes, stirring continuously.
3 Brush on steaks and spareribs before you cook them, and serve the rest with the finished dish.

CREOLE SAUCE
Serves 4

2 tbsp margarine
1×400g (14oz) tin tomato soup
110ml (4floz) water
$\frac{1}{2}$ small green pepper, chopped
1 small onion, chopped
8 stuffed olives, chopped
1 tsp salt

 1 Heat the margarine in a heavy pan.
2 Add all the ingredients and, stirring continuously, cook over a medium heat for 15-20 minutes.
3 Serve this sauce over meat, fish or poultry.

KICK-Y BUTTER
Serves 4

Like a garlic butter, this is really tasty and so nice you'll get a kick each time you taste it.

1tsp chopped chives
1tsp chopped parsley
2 cloves garlic, chopped
$4\frac{1}{2}$ tbsp hot water
75g (3oz) butter
salt and pepper
greaseproof paper

METHOD 1 Boil chives, parsley and garlic in water for 5 minutes. Strain.
3 Blend the herbs with the butter and season to taste.
3 On a board, make into a 2.5cm (1in) diameter roll with the hands. Wrap in wet greaseproof paper and chill in the refrigerator.
4 When hard, cut into slices and use with grilled meat, poultry, fish or vegetables.

HOT PEPPER SAUCE
Serves 2

As it says, this sauce really is *hot!* The Carib Indians were into making it long before Christopher Columbus arrived, and now every Caribbean cook has her own version. This is mine. If you want, you can keep it safely for about 3–4 weeks in a tightly covered container in the refrigerator.

4 tsp chilli peppers, finely chopped
3 cloves garlic, finely chopped
2 small onions, finely chopped
$3\frac{1}{2}$ tbsp malt vinegar
1 tsp salt
4 tbsp water
1 dsp olive oil

METHOD 1 Liquidize all the ingredients together.
2 Bring to the boil in a small enamel, stainless steel or glass saucepan.
3 Stirring all the time, cook gently for 10–15 minutes.

Note Do not forget to be careful when using fresh chillies. They can cause irritation to eyes and skin.

TOMATO CHUTNEY
Makes 12 jars

2.3kg (5lb) green tomatoes
6 large onions
1.4kg (3lb) apples, peeled
1.1l (2pt) vinegar
110g (4oz) salt
15g ($\frac{1}{2}$oz) white pepper
15g ($\frac{1}{2}$oz) cloves
2-3 chillies, de-seeded and
    chopped
900g (2lb) brown sugar
450g (1lb) raisins
peel of 3 lemons, sliced

METHOD 1 Chop tomatoes,
onions and apples.
Place in a deep bowl with all the
other ingredients.
2 Pressure-cook in small
amounts.
3 Combine all together in a large,
heavy saucepan. Bring to the boil
and simmer for 2-3 hours.
4 Put into sterilized jars or bottles
while warm and tie down firmly.

MINT CHUTNEY
Makes 2 jars

This is delicious with various
meats, but especially lamb.

1×275ml ($\frac{1}{2}$pt) measure filled
    with pressed-down mint
    leaves
2 small onions
2 medium cooking apples, cored
225g (8oz) raisins or sultanas
110g (4oz) green or red
    tomatoes, skinned
225g (8oz) soft brown sugar
275ml ($\frac{1}{2}$pt) red wine vinegar
1 tsp dry mustard
1 tsp salt

METHOD 1 Mince all the
ingredients, with the
exception of the mustard and salt.

2 Put into a large pan with 200ml
(7floz) of the vinegar. Bring to
the boil then simmer for 20-25
minutes.
3 Mix the remaining vinegar with
the mustard and salt.
4 Stir into the chutney in the pan
and bring to the boil once more.
Take from the heat and allow to
cool.
5 When cold, pour into pots and
tie down well.

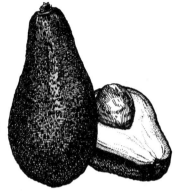

AVOCADO DIP
Serves 4

2 large avocado pears
1 tsp onion, grated
2 tsp lime or lemon juice
4 tbsp mayonnaise
pinch of white pepper
pinch of salt
paprika for garnish

METHOD 1 Cut each avocado
in half, lengthways.
Remove stone.
2 Scoop out the flesh into a bowl
and mash to a paste.
3 Add the remaining ingredients,
except the paprika, and blend
well.
4 Chill in the refrigrator, covered
with cling film.
5 On serving, sprinkle with the
paprika.

'Ebery ho ha hum 'tick a bush.'
Are you having trouble with these
little sayings and proverbs? Not
until you got to this one?
Perhaps it is a bit mysterious-
looking. Just take it slowly and
you get 'Every one stick a bush',
or 'There is a place in life for
everyone.'

FISH AND SEAFOOD

SHARK MUHAMMAD
Serves 4

I created this dish in honour of that great champion boxer, Muhammad Ali, when he came to eat at my restaurant in Birmingham. It is now a speciality of the house. Very rich, it is definitely a dish for a *very* special occasion. To my mind, shark is at least in the same class as salmon. Not only does it taste delicious, you have just the one central bone to worry about; the rest is beautiful firm flesh.

900g (2lb) shark, cut into rounds
2 tsp salt
2 tsp pepper
25g (1oz) butter
1 dsp paprika pepper
1 red, 1 green sweet pepper, chopped
$\frac{1}{4}$ cucumber, chopped
2 tomatoes, chopped
50g (2oz) mushrooms, chopped
1 onion
1 avocado
2 tbsp tomato purée
25g (1oz) plain flour
275ml ($\frac{1}{2}$pt) sweet white wine
225g (8oz) shrimps
175g (6oz) crabmeat
4 oysters
16 langoustines
bunch of parsley and sweet pepper rings for garnish

For each serving, make a bed of callaloo
$\frac{1}{2}$ onion
1 tomato, chopped
knob of butter
1 tin callaloo, cooked
salt and pepper to taste

METHOD 1 Season the shark to taste with the salt and pepper. Grill or pan-fry on each side for about 5 minutes. Keep warm.
2 In a pan, dissolve the butter. Add the paprika, sweet peppers, cucumber, tomatoes, mushrooms and onion and sauté for 4-5 minutes.
3 Peel the avocado, slice and add the flesh to the pan. Cook for a further 2 minutes. Add tomato purée and flour. Stir gently until cooked. Keeping back 57ml (2floz), add the white wine to the pan and allow to simmer for 3-4 minutes, then add the shellfish and allow just to warm through.
4 Grill the oysters with the rest of the white wine under a very low heat until warmed through.
5 Deep-fry the langoustines.
6 To make the callaloo, sauté the chopped onion and tomato in the butter until soft but not brown.
7 Mix in the callaloo, add the salt and pepper and warm through.
8 To serve, form a bed of callaloo on the plate. On top, place a helping of the mixture from the pan. Lay a portion of shark on top. Add the white wine to the juices from the pan and pour over the fish. Place an oyster in the centre, decorate with the langoustines, sweet pepper rings and parsley.

Shark Muhammad

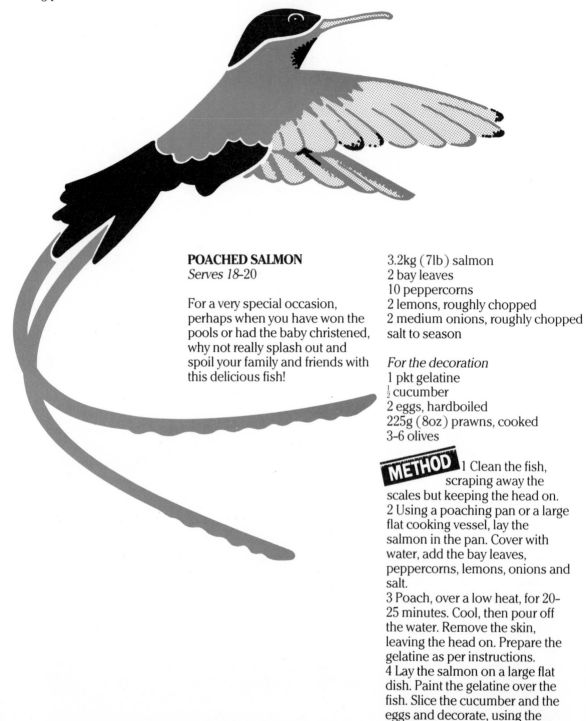

POACHED SALMON
Serves 18-20

For a very special occasion, perhaps when you have won the pools or had the baby christened, why not really splash out and spoil your family and friends with this delicious fish!

3.2kg (7lb) salmon
2 bay leaves
10 peppercorns
2 lemons, roughly chopped
2 medium onions, roughly chopped
salt to season

For the decoration
1 pkt gelatine
½ cucumber
2 eggs, hardboiled
225g (8oz) prawns, cooked
3-6 olives

METHOD 1 Clean the fish, scraping away the scales but keeping the head on.
2 Using a poaching pan or a large flat cooking vessel, lay the salmon in the pan. Cover with water, add the bay leaves, peppercorns, lemons, onions and salt.
3 Poach, over a low heat, for 20-25 minutes. Cool, then pour off the water. Remove the skin, leaving the head on. Prepare the gelatine as per instructions.
4 Lay the salmon on a large flat dish. Paint the gelatine over the fish. Slice the cucumber and the eggs and decorate, using the prawns and olives to your own design.

SNAPPER DELIGHT
Serves 4

Highly valued in the West Indies, the Red Snapper fish is now becoming available in markets over here, and is quite delicious.

4 large red snapper fish, about 225g (8oz) each
2 tsp salt
2 tsp pepper
1 medium onion, grated
oil for frying
50g (2oz) butter
50g (2oz) plain flour
275ml (½pt) milk
275ml (½pt) single cream
4 tbsp sherry
110g (4oz) cheese, grated
4 black olives
parsley for garnish
1 lemon, sliced, for garnish

METHOD 1 Wash and clean the fish (or get your fishmonger to do it for you).
2 Season with the salt, pepper and onion.
3 Pan-fry in the oil for 5 minutes each side then lay the fish in a pie-dish.
4 Rub the butter into the flour. Gently add small balls of this mixture to the milk. Cook to a smooth consistency over a low heat.
5 Stir in the fresh cream and sherry. Pour over the fish, sprinkle with cheese and place an olive in the eye of each fish.
6 Bake at 190°C (375°F) Reg 5 for 15-20 minutes. Garnish with parsley and lemon slices.
See illustration on page 37

ACKEE AND SALT FISH
Serves 4

Almost the national dish of Jamaica (and the Queen's favourite when she visits the Caribbean), this is one of the finest dishes around! Ackee grows on a tree and is the flesh found in the seed pods.

450g (1lb) salt fish (cod)
1×425g (15oz) tin ackee
110g (4oz) margarine
2 rashers of bacon, chopped
1 large onion, chopped
2 medium tomatoes, chopped
1 medium sweet pepper, chopped
½ tsp thyme
black pepper and salt to taste
parsley for garnish

METHOD 1 Boil the fish for 10 minutes or, alternatively, soak overnight.
2 Wash to remove excess salt, remove the skin and bones and flake the fish.
3 Open the tin of ackee and drain.
4 Melt the margarine in a pan and gently fry the bacon for 3 minutes.
5 Add the onion, tomatoes and sweet pepper to the pan together with the thyme.
6 Cook for a further 5 minutes, stirring gently. Add the fish, blackpepper and salt and cook for 10 minutes.
7 Add the ackee and cook for 8-10 minutes, turning gently.
8 Garnish with the parsley. Serve with Rice and Gungo Peas (see Vegetable Dishes).
See illustration on page 37

'Carry me ackee, go a Linstead Market
Not a quattie wud sell.'
(Traditional song)

35

Fish and Seafood

ESCOVEITCH FISH
Serves 4

The name probably comes from the Spanish, *escabeche*, which is a traditional cooking method used throughout Latin America. It consists of a marinade of spices and vinegar which is poured over fish, usually goatfish, snapper or herrings. It is a very popular dish in Jamaica and deserves to be just as popular elsewhere. This is how I make it:

1.8kg (4lb) whole fish – herrings, goatfish, snapper, etc, as preferred
25g (1oz) pimento seeds (optional)
50g (2oz) peppercorns
2 chilli peppers, de-seeded and chopped
$\frac{1}{2}$ each of red and green sweet pepper, de-seeded and chopped
2 onions, chopped
2 cloves garlic, chopped
275ml ($\frac{1}{2}$pt) vinegar
1 tsp salt
1 tsp pepper
oil for frying

METHOD 1 Wash and clean the fish, keeping the heads on. Lay flat on a dish.
2 Mix together all the ingredients, except the oil and vinegar, and season the fish with them.
3 Pour over the vinegar and leave to marinate overnight.
4 Remove the fish from the marinade. Fry, either in deep or shallow oil, for about 8 minutes.
5 Bring the marinade to the boil in a saucepan and cook for 10 minutes.
6 When cooked, lay the fish on a serving dish and pour over the marinade.
7 Serve with deep-fried Dumplin's (see recipe with Jerk Pork).

STAMP AND GO
Serves 6–8

These salt fish fritters are a traditional dish of Jamaica. It has been suggested that the name came about because of the island people's liking for all things nautical. 'Stamp and go' was a seventeenth-century command to English sailors when they had to haul on a line or turn the capstan. It seems that the phrase just stuck! Another odd explanation is that customers asking for the fritters in a shop would 'stamp' their feet to get attention, and 'go' if they did not receive it!

As saltfish is used, you must remember to de-salt it by soaking overnight in cold water. Cook by covering with fresh, cold water, bring to the boil and simmer for about 15 minutes. Skin and flake before use.

1 small onion
1 chilli, de-seeded
110g (4oz) butter or margarine, melted
450g (1 lb) self-raising flour
1 tsp salt
275ml ($\frac{1}{2}$pt) water
225g (8oz) cooked saltfish, or fresh cod if you prefer

METHOD 1 Chop the onion and chilli finely. Rub the margarine, flour and salt together.
2 Make a well in the mixture. Using the water, make a thick batter, beating well.
3 Add the flaked fish to the batter together with the onions and chillies. Allow to stand for 10 minutes.
4 Heat the oil. Drop in large spoonfuls of the batter and fry for 4–5 minutes each side until golden brown. Serve hot.

'If you no done cross riber, no t'row 'way you 'tick.'

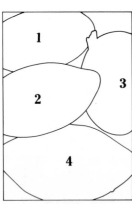

1 Snapper Delight 2 Ackee and Salt Fish 3 Escoveitch Fish
4 Stamp and Go

COD FISH, PINEAPPLE AND RICE
Serves 4

225g (8oz) cod, grilled or braised
    in a little milk and butter,
    seasoned to taste
450g (1lb) long-grain rice,
    cooked
225g (8oz) prawns, cooked and
    peeled
110ml (4fl oz) vinaigrette (oil and
    vinegar dressing)
salt and pepper
2 medium pineapples
red pepper, lettuce and tomato
    for decoration

METHOD 1 Roughly flake the
cod, and add to the
rice in a bowl with half the
prawns, a little vinaigrette and

seasoning to taste.
2 Halve the pineapples
lengthways, scoop out the flesh
and chop it roughly.
3 Mix with the fish and rice and
put back into the pineapple
'shells'.
4 Decorate with the remaining
prawns, strips of red pepper and
tomato on a bed of lettuce leaves.

CUTTLEFISH STARTER
Serves 6–8

There are so many different fish
appearing in our supermarkets
these days, why not try something
very different – like cuttlefish?
This member of the squid family
is really tasty.

1.4kg (3lb) cuttlefish
3 tbsp olive oil
2 cloves garlic, chopped
$\frac{1}{2}$ medium sweet pepper,
    de-seeded and chopped
2 tsp chilli powder
1×400g (14oz) tin tomatoes
350g (12oz) sweetcorn
salt and pepper to season
1 glass white wine

METHOD 1 Ask your
fishmonger to clean
the fish for you. (The bone comes
in very handy for the budgie!)
2 Wash thoroughly. Peel away the
outer skin and discard.
3 Cut the fish into 6mm ($\frac{1}{4}$in)
strips and fry gently in the olive oil
until tender.
4 Add all the ingredients except
the wine and cook for about 30
minutes. Cool slightly and add
the wine.

FISH PANCAKES
Serves 2

For the pancakes
175g (6oz) plain flour
1 egg
275ml ($\frac{1}{2}$pt) milk
pinch of salt
oil for frying

For the filling
oil for frying
1 large onion
450g (1lb) white fish, cooked and
    flaked
175g (6oz) shrimps
2 large tomatoes, chopped
1 tsp chilli powder
salt and pepper to taste
8 large prawns for decoration

Sauce for filling
25g (1oz) plain flour
25g (1oz) butter
275ml ($\frac{1}{2}$pt) milk
salt and pepper to taste
1 small tin tomatoes

METHOD 1 To make the
pancakes, sieve the
flour into a bowl. Make a well in
the centre and add the egg.
2 Add the milk slowly, season

with the salt, and mix to a smooth
batter.
3 Leave to stand for 10 minutes.
4 Heat the oil in a heavy pan and
fry the pancakes, using enough
batter just to cover the base of the
pan. Remember to toss them with
care!
5 Heat the oil and gently fry the
onion for 5-8 minutes. Add the
fish, shrimps, tomatoes, chilli
powder and salt and pepper. Fry
for a further 8-10 minutes.
6 Prepare the sauce by mixing the
flour, butter, milk, salt and
pepper, then add the tin of
tomatoes.
7 Add the fish mixture to the
sauce, saving a little to pour over
the pancakes.
8 Put fish mixture into each
pancake and pop into a warm
oven for 10 minutes.
9 Decorate with the prawns. (You
can also use chopped chives or
parsley.)
See illustration on page 41

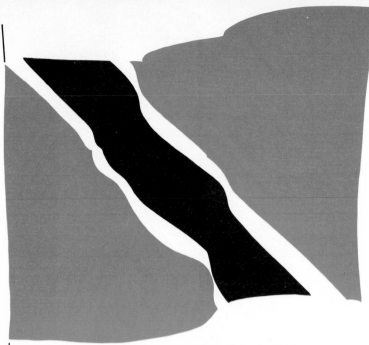

PRAWN PINEAPPLE PORT OF SPAIN
Serves 2

350g (12oz) peeled prawns
    (keep a few for decoration)
strained juice of 1 lime
2 tbsp olive oil
1 onion, peeled and chopped
3 tbsp chives, chopped
1 shallot, peeled and chopped
2 tomatoes, peeled and chopped
2 tbsp curry powder
275ml ($\frac{1}{2}$pt) water
25g (1oz) plain flour
25g (1oz) butter
2 small pineapples

METHOD 1 Soak the prawns in the lime juice for 30 minutes.
2 Heat the oil. Fry the onion, 1 tsp chives, shallot, tomatoes and curry powder for 5 minutes without browning.
3 Add the water and simmer for about 15 minutes.
4 Remove from the heat. Rub the flour into the butter and add small amounts to the pan, stirring continuously until thickened. Cook for 3 minutes.
5 Cut the pineapples in half, lengthways, cutting through the leaves. Remove the hard core at the centre and discard. Scoop out the flesh.
6 Chop the flesh and add to the pan along with the prawns. Cook for about 6–8 minutes, stirring continuously.
7 Grill the pineapple 'shells'. Fill with the mixture, sprinkle with the remaining chopped chives and garnish with a few prawns.

PRAWN STUFFED PEPPERS
Serves 4

8 medium-sized green peppers
175g (6oz) prawns, chopped
350g (12oz) long-grain rice,
    cooked
3 medium tomatoes, chopped
1 medium onion, chopped
1 clove garlic, crushed
2 tsp thyme
3 tsp parsley, chopped
150ml ($\frac{1}{4}$pt) fish stock

METHOD 1 With a sharp knife, cut away the stalk from each pepper, then cut off and keep the tops.
2 De-seed each pepper, then stand them in a deep, ovenproof dish.
3 Mix together all the other ingredients, except the stock, and stuff the peppers well.
4 Replace the top on each pepper and pour the stock around them in the dish.
5 Bake at 190°C (375°F) Reg 5 for 30–40 minutes.
6 Garnish with parsley.

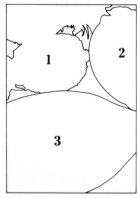

1 Prawn Pineapple Port of Spain
2 Prawn Stuffed Peppers 3 Fish
Pancakes

'Darg don' nyam darg.'

SHRIMP SOUFFLÉ
Serves 4

225g (8oz) peeled shrimps
65g (2½oz) butter
1 small onion, finely chopped
6 tbsp plain flour
275ml (½pt) milk
juice of 1 lemon
1 tsp grated nutmeg
salt and pepper
6 eggs, separated

METHOD 1 Wash shrimps and chop finely. Melt the butter in a heavy pan.
2 Add the onion and cook for 4–5 minutes. Add the flour and mix in well.
3 Gently add the milk, a little at a time, stirring until the mixture thickens.
4 Add the lemon juice, nutmeg and seasoning. Remove from the heat and stir in the lightly beaten egg yolks.
5 Beat the egg whites till stiff. Stir half the quantity into the shrimp mixture, then fold in the other half very gently.
6 Pour into a slightly greased soufflé dish and bake at 190°C (375°F) Reg 5 for 35–40 minutes until golden and light.
7 Serve at once!

PRAWNS IN MELON
Serves 1

1 medium-sized melon
175g (6oz) peeled prawns
2 tbsp tomato ketchup
5 tbsp single cream
6 tbsp mayonnaise
1 small green pepper, de-seeded and chopped
salt and pepper
parsley for garnish

METHOD 1 Slice the top off the melon. Scoop out the seeds and flesh. Put the 'shell' and the prawns into the refrigerator to chill.
2 Mix the tomato ketchup, cream, mayonnaise and chopped pepper together and season.
3 Cut the melon flesh into cubes and add to the sauce. Chill. When cold, mix with the prawns, fill the melon shell, sprinkle with parsley and serve on a bed of cracked ice.

STUFFED AVOCADOS
Serves 4

1×225g (8oz) tin tuna fish
1 small onion, finely chopped
1 clove garlic (optional)
$\frac{1}{4}$ cucumber, finely chopped
a few sprigs of parsley, finely
        chopped
2 tbsp mayonnaise
4 avocados
juice of 1 lime
lettuce, tomato and extra parsley
        for garnish

METHOD 1 Mix together the flaked tuna fish, onion, garlic if liked, cucumber, parsley and mayonnaise.
2 Halve the avocados, remove the stones and brush the exposed flesh with lime juice to stop discoloration.
3 Fill the hollows with the tuna fish mixture.
4 Place on individual dishes, surrounded by lettuce and tomato slices, garnished with extra parsley, and serve immediately.

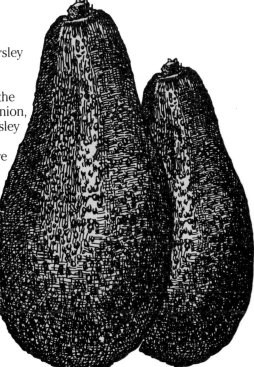

MEAT

SPICY BEEF RINGS
Serves 2

4 ripe plantains
50g (2oz) butter
vegetable oil for frying

For the filling
450g (1lb) lean minced beef
1 small green pepper, de-seeded
    and finely chopped
2 small onions, finely chopped
1 large tomato, skinned and finely
    chopped
2 tbsp tomato purée
2 tbsp vegetable oil
2 tsp salt
2 tsp pepper
110g (4oz) sweetcorn
parsley for garnish

METHOD 1 Blend all the filling
ingredients together in
a bowl.
2 Heat the oil in a heavy pan and
fry for 15 minutes. Keep warm.
3 Peel and cut the plantains. Slice
lengthways.

4 Pan-fry in butter for about 5
minutes.
5 Remove from the pan. Curve
each plantain slice round to form
a ring and secure with a cocktail
stick.
6 Place plantain rings on a baking
tray. Spoon the mixture into the
centre of each, filling to the top.
7 Bake at 190°C (375°F) Reg 5 for
15–20 minutes.
8 Garnish with parsley and serve
with rice and peas (as below).

For the rice and peas
1×425g (15oz) can red kidney
    beans or 225g (8oz) red
    peas
450g (1lb) white Patna rice
    (cleaned)
$\frac{1}{2}$ small onion, chopped
    water
    salt

METHOD 1 If the peas are the
dry red sort, soak them
overnight in cold water. Then
cook them with salt for at least 1
hour until they are soft. Make sure
that the water is always approx.
2.5cm (1in) above the peas.
2 Add the rice and onion to the
peas and the liquid and bring to
the boil, stirring continuously.
Then lower the heat until it is
simmering for about 35–40
minutes. The rice and peas will
then be perfectly lovely.
3 If you use the canned peas, add
the juice in the can to about
275ml ($\frac{1}{2}$pt) water and cook the
peas in the same way.

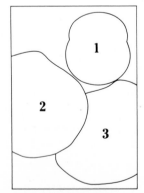

1 Mutton Devil Creek **2** Super
Stuffed Beef **3** Spicy Beef Rings

SUPER STUFFED BEEF
Serves 6

1.6kg (3½lb) brisket
2 carrots, peeled
salt and pepper to season
1 large onion
110ml (4fl oz) olive oil
2 German sausages or salamis
1 bottle red wine
50g (2oz) plain flour

METHOD 1 Lay meat flat on a
board and cut almost
through lengthways.
2 Open out meat and lay carrots,
whole, along length. Season with
salt and pepper. Sweat the onions
in the olive oil.
3 Cut a V shape out of each
sausage, and lay them V side
down, over the carrots.
4 Roll meat up into a round and
tie well with string. Place in a
deep roasting tin.
5 Pour sweated onion over the
meat, cover with bottle of wine
(keeping a small glass for
yourself if your spirits are
flagging!) and cook for 3 hours in
a slow oven at 180°C (350°F) Reg 4.
6 Thicken the sauce in the pan
with flour and pour over the meat
when serving.
See illustration on page 45

BEEF WELLINGTON
A LA RUSTIE
Serves 4-6

Said to have been created for the
Duke of Wellington after the Battle
of Waterloo, this is a classic dish,
but you don't have to belong to the
'upper crust' to enjoy its delights.

1.1kg (2½lb) fillet steak (in one
piece)
50g (2oz) butter
1 large onion, chopped
225g (8oz) mushrooms,
chopped small
1 pkt frozen puff pastry
110g (4oz) duck pâté
1 egg
2 cloves garlic, chopped
salt and pepper to taste

METHOD 1 Gently fry the
steak in the butter, and
sweat down the onions, garlic
and mushrooms.
2 Roll the pastry out into an
oblong, long enough and wide
enough to cover meat and seal.
3 Spread the onion and
mushroom mixture over the
pastry, place the steak in the
centre, season with salt and
pepper and spread the duck pâté
over the meat.
4 Beat the egg and brush over the
edges of the pastry. Fold
over the meat to make a
parcel and seal the edges.
Brush over with the beaten egg.
5 Place on a greased baking sheet.
Make 2 cuts in the pastry
and decorate with pastry flower
and leaf shapes.
6 Bake at 220°C (425°F) Reg 7 for
35-40 minutes, less if you like
your meat rare. Serve hot or cold.

SAVOURY BEEF PIE
Serves 4

A very quick, tasty pie, ideal for lunch or supper, and not unlike a Shepherd's Pie except this one's got some extra flavours to give it bite.

For the topping
900g (2lb) sweet potato
900g (2lb) potatoes
110g (4oz) butter
57ml (2fl oz) milk
2 tsp white pepper to season
50g (2oz) cheese, grated, for
    garnish
parsley for garnish

For the filling
110ml (4fl oz) vegetable oil
900g (2lb) minced beef
225g (8oz) onions, minced
1 dsp black pepper
1 tsp chilli pepper
1 dsp salt
1×400g (14oz) tin tomatoes
1×400g (14oz) tin red kidney
    beans

METHOD 1 Peel boil and mash the potatoes, using the butter, milk and white pepper. Set aside, keeping warm.
2 Heat the vegetable oil and gently fry the minced beef and onions together, until tender.
3 Add the other ingredients to the pan, stir in well and heat through.
4 Put the mixture into a pie dish. Pipe over the mashed potatoes, sprinkle with grated cheese, and brown under a hot grill. Garnish with parsley.

BEEF CURRY
Serves 4

In this recipe I specify Madras curry powder because I like my Beef Curry to come out hot and strong. A lot of the time, though, it is really up to you to decide which curry powder you prefer. There are so many to choose from, and another thing that interests me is their colour range and the different visual effects that you can create. By and large a Caribbean curry is milder than an Indian curry, and its success depends mainly on how you combine the various spices and other flavours until you reach the balance that you feel is right for you.

900g (2lb) shin of beef
75g (3oz) plain flour
2 dsp Madras curry powder
2 tsp salt
2 tsp ginger
2 tsp chilli powder
2 bay leaves, crumbled
oil to fry
1 clove garlic, chopped
2 medium onions, chopped
2 tbsp tomato purée

METHOD 1 Cube meat and trim away any fat.
2 Put the dry ingredients in a bowl and roll the meat in them.
3 Heat oil and fry meat for 10 minutes to seal.
4 Add the garlic, onions and tomato purée to the pan and cook on a low heat for about $1\frac{1}{2}$ hours until tender, stirring frequently.
5 Serve on a bed of rice.

PEPPERED STEAK CARIBBEAN
Serves 2

450g (1lb) sirloin steak
1 tsp salt
1 tsp black pepper
110ml (4floz) French mustard
110g (4oz) ground peppercorns
oil to fry
peppers and salad for garnish

For the white sauce
25g (1oz) plain flour
275ml (½pt) milk
110ml (4floz) sweet sherry
110ml (4floz) cream

METHOD 1 Beat steak flat. Season with salt and pepper. Spread with French mustard.
2 Dip in the peppercorns and coat each side.
3 Heat the oil and fry the steak for 5–8 minutes each side. Remove from the pan.
4 To make the sauce, mix the flour and milk together and add them to the juice in the pan.
5 Add the cream and sherry and gently mix in. Bring to the boil and allow to thicken.
6 Arrange the steaks on a plate or dish, and pour over the sauce.
7 Garnish with peppers and salad, serve with rice and gungo peas.

JERK PORK AND DUMPLIN'S
Serves 6–8

Jerk pork was introduced from Africa, where the men had been hunters. For their long journeys, they took a whole pig and cleaned and stuffed it with seasonings and blood. This they cooked over hot coals; the meat lasted for several weeks, so was very useful. Today, the men who prepare and sell this delicious meat in the market squares are called the 'Jerk Men'. When I went to Africa, I saw and bought jerk, so the old traditions are being carried on.

1 tsp mixed spice
1 dsp chilli powder
1 dsp paprika
2 tsp cinnamon
1 tsp salt
½ small sweet pepper, red and green, chopped
1 medium onion, chopped
1.8kg (4lb) joint of pork
57ml (2floz) clear honey
50g (2oz) soft brown sugar
1 bay leaf
20 cloves (optional)

For the dumplin's
450g (1lb) plain flour
1 tsp baking powder
1 tsp salt
25g (1oz) margarine
water to bind
oil for frying

METHOD 1 Put all the dry ingredients, except the cloves and bay leaf, into a bowl. Add the peppers and onions and combine well.
2 Make a hole in the meat. Stuff the mixture into the meat. Place in a baking tin, pour over the honey and sprinkle with the brown sugar.
3 If using cloves, push in decoratively over the surface of the meat.
4 Bake for 3 hours at 190°C (375°F) Reg 5.
5 To make the dumplin's, put all the dry ingredients into a bowl, rub in the fat and bind together with the water.
6 Heat the oil, roll the mixture into balls and deep-fry until 'fluffy'.
7 Drain and serve.

'Cap no fit you, you no tek up.'

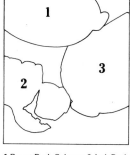

1 Roast Pork Calypso 2 Jerk Pork and Dumplin's 3 Rustie's Saucy Spareribs

BEEF STROGANOFF A LA RUSTIE
Serves 2

Traditionally, this famous classic dish uses fillet steak as its main ingredient, but if your purse won't stretch to that, don't worry, because this recipe of mine will still give you a superb meal.

75g (3oz) plain flour
2 tsp paprika
2 tsp salt
2 tsp black pepper
50g (2oz) butter
450g (1lb) chuck steak
575ml (1pt) beef stock
2 small onions, chopped
110g (4oz) mushrooms
150ml (5fl oz) soured cream

METHOD 1 Mix all the dry ingredients together. Heat the butter in a heavy pan.
2 Cut the meat into cubes and coat in the seasoned flour. Fry in the butter, 5 minutes each side. Remove from the pan and keep warm.
3 Return the meat to the pan, add the beef stock and onions, cover and cook for 1 hour on a low heat.
4 Add the mushrooms and the soured cream. Simmer for a further 30 minutes.
5 Serve with boiled rice or jacket potatoes.

'Two darg fe one bone, two 'ooman fe one house, neber 'gree lang.'

SPICY BEEF WITH OLIVES AND RAISINS
Serves 4

1.1kg (2½lb) chuck beef
3 tsp salt
2 tsp pepper
6 tbsp vegetable oil
1 large onion, finely chopped
2 cloves garlic, finely chopped
2-3 fresh chillies, de-seeded and finely chopped
450g (1lb) tomatoes, peeled, de-seeded and finely chopped
75g (3oz) stuffed green olives
50g (2oz) seedless raisins
2 tbsp distilled white vinegar

METHOD 1 Trim excess fat from the meat and cut into 5cm (2in) cubes.
2 Place in a large, heavy saucepan and season well with half the salt and pepper. Add enough water to well cover the meat.
3 Bring to the boil rapidly and skim. Lower the heat, partly cover the pan and simmer for 2 hours until the meat is tender. Remove from the pan.
4 Heat oil over a moderate heat. Drop in the onion, garlic and chillies. Cook for about 5 minutes, stirring continuously, until the vegetables are soft but not brown.
5 Add the tomatoes, season with the rest of the salt and pepper. Cook for 5 minutes then add the olives, raisins and vinegar. Stir well.
6 Return the beef to the pan and heat through. Taste for seasoning and serve with rice, gungo peas and tomato salad.

CARIBBEAN BEEF STEW

Serves 4

1–2 cloves garlic, crushed
25g (1oz) plain flour, mixed with
      salt, pepper and 2 tsp paprika
450g (1lb) stewing beef, cubed
1 large onion, peeled and sliced
2 tbsp oil
225g (8oz) red kidney beans,
      soaked overnight and
      cooked for 1 hour
a few sprigs of thyme
2–3 chillies
50g (2oz) creamed coconut
      (see recipe at end of
      Puddings and Sweets)
900g (2lb) mixed prepared
      vegetables (pumpkin,
      sweet potato, yam, chow-
      chow, green bananas)

METHOD 1 Rub the garlic and
flour into the meat.
Leave for 1 hour.
2 Fry the onion in the oil. Add the
meat and stir until well browned.
3 Add beans and 600–850ml (1–
$1\frac{1}{2}$pt) of their liquid, the thyme,
chillies and creamed coconut.
4 Bring the mixture to the boil,
stirring until liquid thickens
slightly. Cover and cook very
slowly for about $2\frac{1}{2}$ hours, adding
the vegetables after about $1\frac{1}{2}$
hours.

Note Be careful not to overcook
the vegetables.

'No ebery t'ing wha' hab sugar
sweet.'

ROAST PORK CALYPSO
Serves 6-8

Try roasting your pork joint this way for a really delicious change.

2.7kg (6lb) lean pork loin
    (preferably the middle cut)
1 pkt (570ml) chicken stock
225g (8oz) brown sugar
28ml (1fl oz) clear honey
$2\frac{1}{2}$ tsp garlic, finely chopped
$1\frac{1}{2}$ tsp ground ginger, or
    25g (1oz) root ginger,
    peeled and grated
$2\frac{1}{2}$ tbsp dark rum
1 bay leaf, crumbled
2 tsp salt
2 tsp black pepper
3 tbsp light rum
1 dsp cornflour, blended with 4
    tsp cold water
$2\frac{1}{2}$ tbsp strained, fresh lemon juice

METHOD 1 Pre-heat oven to 180°C (350°F) Reg 4. Lightly score the skin of the pork with a sharp knife.

2 Place, skin side up, in a shallow roasting tin. Roast in the top of the oven for $1\frac{3}{4}$ hours, until golden brown.

3 Remove from the tin and place on a dish. Skim fat from the pan and add stock.

4 Mix the sugar, garlic, ginger, dark rum, bay leaf, salt and pepper in a bowl, using the back of a spoon.

5 Spread this mixture over the scored side of the pork with a knife. Place the meat back in the tin, fat side up, and roast for another 30 minutes until the top is crunchy and brown. Transfer to a serving dish.

6 Warm the light rum in a small pan over a low heat. Set alight off the heat, with a match, moving the pan to and fro until the flame dies away.

7 Bring the liquid from the roasting tin to a quick boil. Blend the cornflour and add this to the pan, stirring constantly until thickened.

8 Remove from the heat, stir in the flamed rum and lemon juice. Use as sauce.

See illustration on page 48

'Neber buy puss in a bag.'
(Or, while we're in the Pork department, a pig in a poke!)

RUSTIE'S SAUCY SPARERIBS
Serves 4

Spareribs are very popular in the Caribbean. Meat is expensive over there and people use as many parts of the animal as they can – from Pigtail Soup all the way up to the front!

1.8kg (4lb) spareribs of pork
2 medium onions, chopped
1 dsp salt
1 dsp ginger
2 cloves garlic, crushed
1 tsp red colouring
170ml (6fl oz) clear honey
225g (8oz) brown sugar
2 tbsp tomato ketchup
275ml ($\frac{1}{2}$pt) vinegar
57ml (2fl oz) soy sauce
1.1–1.4 l (2–2$\frac{1}{2}$pt) water
cornflour to thicken
lemon and parsley for garnish

 1 Separate the spareribs and put into a deep, ovenproof dish.
2 Add all the other ingredients and turn the meat in them, coating all over and mixing well.
3 Cook in a slow oven at 160°C (325°F) Reg 3 for 2–2$\frac{1}{2}$ hours.
4 Thicken the sauce with a little cornflour during the last 20 minutes of cooking time. Garnish with lemon wedges or slices and parsley.
See illustration on page 48

BOOZY PORK
Serves 2

4 pork chops
1 small onion, chopped
1 medium cooking apple,
    roughly chopped
2 dsp cornflour
oil for frying

For the marinade
2 tsp ginger
1 tsp cinnamon
1 tsp chilli pepper
1 tsp ground pepper
1 can lager beer

METHOD 1 To make the marinade, put the spices in a bowl and mix together.
2 Coat the chops with this mixture, then add the apple and onion.
3 Pour over the lager and marinate overnight.
4 Fry chops 5 minutes each side to seal, then combine with the liquor, apple and onion in the pan. Cover with a tight-fitting lid and cook over a low heat for 30 minutes.
5 Mix the cornflour with a little water, add to the pan, and cook for a further 10 minutes.

'Cuss-cuss no bore 'ole in me 'kin.'

MUTTON DEVIL CREEK
Serves 4

900g (2lb) leg of mutton, cut into
    5cm (2in) cubes
2 cloves garlic, finely chopped
2 onions, chopped
2 carrots, peeled and chopped
2 tsp salt
2 tsp black pepper
2 tsp thyme
2 dsp curry powder (Madras)
3 tbsp oil, for frying
1 tbsp granulated sugar
1.1l (2pt) water
2 tbsp tomato purée
2 chilli peppers
2 tbsp plain flour dissolved in
    cold water for thickening

METHOD 1 Season the meat with the chopped garlic, onion, carrot, salt, pepper, thyme and curry powder. Really press the seasoning into the meat. This can be left overnight to marinate.
2 Put the oil into the frying pan and heat until very hot. Add the granulated sugar and allow to caramelize. Then add the meat pieces and fry for 10 minutes, turning occasionally.
3 Take the oil away. Put the meat and juice into a saucepan with the 1.1l (2pt) water, tomato purée and the chilli pepper (scored but whole) and cook for 1 hour on a low heat. Then stir occasionally and add the rest of the seasoning. Cook for a further 20–25 minutes.
4 Remove the chilli pepper and add the thickening (flour and water). Cook for a further 10 minutes. Serve on a bed of rice.
See illustration on page 45

LAMB WINO
Serves 4

Don't mind some of the titles I give my dishes! This one is just a nice way of doing lamb chops with wine, but somebody thought it meant you had to run after a little lamb and then get him so drunk he didn't care if you cooked him or not. I had to laugh, of course, but Rustie would never do a terrible thing like that…Honestly!

1tsp paprika
3 bay leaves
1tbsp parsley, finely chopped
3 cloves (optional)
1.4kg (3lb) lamb leg chops
1 bottle red wine
1 medium onion, chopped
25g (1oz) plain flour
water to mix

METHOD 1 Put all the dry ingredients into a bowl, mix together and well coat the chops.
2 Add the onion. Pour over the bottle of red wine and leave to marinate for 24 hours.
3 Place the chops and marinade in an ovenproof dish and cook for 1 hour at 180°C (350°F) Reg 4.
4 Turn the chops over once during the cooking, add more wine if necessary, and remove any fat by skimming. Thicken the sauce with the flour and water.

LAMB AND SWEET PEPPER CASSEROLE
Serves 4

110g (4oz) red kidney beans
8 lamb chops
3 medium onions, chopped
50g (2oz) margarine
1tsp cooking oil
3 medium sweet green peppers, chopped
225g (8oz) tin tomatoes
salt and pepper
chicken stock cube
275ml ($\frac{1}{2}$pt) boiling water

METHOD 1 Soak the beans overnight. Cook for at least 45 minutes.
2 Grill the chops at full heat for 6–8 minutes each side.
3 Fry the onions in the margarine and oil until soft. Add the green peppers and cook for a further 4–5 minutes.
4 Add the tomatoes, salt and pepper. Dissolve the chicken stock cube in the boiling water.
5 Put the chops in a shallow ovenproof dish, pour over the 'sauce' and bake at 180°C (350°F) Reg 4 for 25–30 minutes.

RUSTIE'S IRISH STEW
Serves 4

Strange though it may seem, there is a strong Irish influence in the Caribbean – and it's not just through the Guinness, which is very popular as an iced drink. I myself have Irish ancestors somewhere up in my family tree, so it is possible that they brought this stew over with them all those years ago.

1 large onion
2 large carrots
3 large potatoes
450g (1lb) stewing lamb
1 dsp salt
1 dsp pepper
1 dsp sugar
$\frac{1}{2}$ can Guinness
575ml (1pt) stock or water
3 dsp tomato purée
2 tsp parsley
2 tsp thyme
25g (1oz) plain flour or cornflour to thicken

METHOD 1 Peel all vegetables and chop.
2 Put the meat in a pan with salt, pepper and sugar and cook for 5 minutes. Stir continuously.
3 Add onion and carrots and stir well.
4 Pour on the Guinness and the stock or water. Add the potatoes and tomato purée and cook for 45 minutes over a low heat, with the lid on.
5 Mix the flour or cornflour with a little water. Add to the stew with the parsley and thyme. Stir in well, cover and cook for a further 15 minutes.

POULTRY

CHICKEN IN A 'OLE
Serves 2

225g (8oz) minced chicken
2 tbsp parsley, finely chopped
2 tsp garlic, finely chopped
1 onion, grated
2 dsp curry powder
1 tsp salt
1 tsp black pepper
50g (2oz) French mustard
2 eggs, beaten
4 tbsp golden breadcrumbs
deep oil for frying

METHOD 1 Mix the chicken
with the parsley, garlic,
onion, curry powder, salt and
pepper.
2 Bind with the mustard and form
into balls.
3 Roll in the beaten egg and
breadcrumbs and leave in the
refrigerator for about 30 minutes
to 'firm up.'
4 Fry the balls in deep fat for
about 8 minutes.
5 Serve on sticks,
very hot!

CHICKEN SURPRISE
Serves 3

I expect you are wondering what
the surprise is. I'll tell you. There's
no rum in it!

350g (12oz) wheat macaroni
3 chicken breasts, boned and
        skinned
1 tsp salt
1 tsp black pepper
$\frac{1}{2}$ tsp thyme
57ml (2fl oz) vegetable oil
25g (1oz) butter
25g (1oz) plain flour
275ml ($\frac{1}{2}$pt) milk
110g (4oz) grated cheese
parsley for garnish
$\frac{1}{2}$ tsp paprika

METHOD 1 Boil the macaroni
for 10 minutes.
2 Season the chicken with the
salt, pepper and thyme.
3 Fry the chicken in the oil for 6–7
minutes each side.
4 Make a white sauce, using the
butter, flour and milk.
5 Place the macaroni in a dish
and put the chicken on top. Cover
with the white sauce.
6 Sprinkle with grated cheese and
bake in a moderate oven at 180°C
(350°F) Reg 4 for 10–15 minutes
or until golden brown.
7 Garnish with parsley, sprinkle
with paprika and serve with
baked potatoes, sweetcorn and
peas.

CHICKEN 'RUN-DUN' (RUN-DOWN)
Serves 4

Why not serve this dish in the coconut shells? Your guests will love this novel touch.

900g (2lb) chicken
110g (4oz) butter
1 coconut, grated
575ml (1pt) water
110ml (4fl oz) fresh cream
110ml (4fl oz) coconut liqueur
    such as Malibu (optional)

For the seasoning
25g (1oz) plain flour
2 tsp ginger
2 tsp thyme
2 tsp black pepper

For the sauce
25g (1oz) plain flour
25g (1oz) butter

METHOD 1 Cut the chicken into pieces and add the seasoning.
2 Fry the chicken in butter for 10-12 minutes.
3 Grate the coconut, squeeze it through the water, then strain.
4 Pour this liquid onto the chicken and allow to cook for a further 15 minutes (approx).
5 While this is cooking, make the sauce. Mix together the flour and butter and roll into small balls, and add these, one by one, stirring gently.
6 Add the fresh cream and the coconut liqueur. Stir in and cook for another 10-12 minutes.
See illustration on page 65

Poultry

58

ORANGEY CHICKEN
Serves 4

4 chicken pieces
1 tsp salt
1 tsp pepper
40g (1½oz) lard
1½ tsp vegetable oil
25g (1oz) plain flour
½ tsp cinnamon
½ tsp ginger
275ml (½pt) orange juice
50g (2oz) blanched almonds

METHOD 1 Season the chicken pieces with the salt and pepper. Heat the lard and oil together and fry until the skins are golden brown. Remove the chicken pieces and keep warm.
2 Into the pan put the flour, cinnamon and ginger. Cook for 2–3 minutes, stirring all the time.
3 Add the orange juice to the pan. Stir in well. Bring to the boil stirring all the time. Add the almonds.
4 Replace the chicken pieces. Cover the pan tightly and simmer for 40 minutes.
5 Serve on a bed of rice and garnish with orange segments or slices.

CARIBBEAN CHICKEN
Serves 4

1 medium red sweet pepper
1 medium green sweet pepper
50g (2oz) butter
salt and pepper
1 tsp cinnamon
4 chicken breasts, skinned and boned
plain flour to coat chicken
cocktail sticks
oil for frying

For the batter
110g (4oz) self-raising flour
1 egg
salt and pepper
1 small tin sweetcorn
275ml (½pt) milk

METHOD 1 Cut the peppers into strips and sweat down in the heated butter.
2 Season with salt, pepper and cinnamon.
3 Dry the chicken breasts and rub over with the flour. Make a slit in one side of each breast and stuff 3 pepper strips into the slit. Secure with a cocktail stick pushed through the flesh.
4 To make the batter, put the flour in a bowl and add the egg, salt, pepper and milk. Mix to a smooth batter. Add the sweetcorn and mix in.
5 Dip each chicken breast in the batter and coat well. Fry in hot oil for 8 minutes.

CHICKEN AND RICE STEW
Serves 4

1.4kg (3lb) chicken, cut into 8
    pieces
2 cloves garlic, chopped
1 large onion, finely chopped
2 dsp freshly ground black pepper
4 tbsp salt
75g (3oz) green and red peppers,
    chopped
1 tbsp curry powder
2 tsp cinnamon
2 tsp nutmeg
85ml (3fl oz) vegetable oil
1 dsp brown sugar
450g (1lb) long-grain white rice
1.7l (3pt) chicken stock
4 tomatoes, peeled, seeded and
    chopped
225g (8oz) garden peas

METHOD 1 Skin the chicken.
2 Into a bowl put the
garlic, onion, black pepper, salt,
sweet peppers, curry powder,
cinnamon and nutmeg. Mix
together well.
3 Coat the chicken by turning in
this mixture. (The chicken can be
left in it overnight if desired.)
4 Heat the oil and add the sugar.
Allow it to dissolve. Fry the
chicken pieces until golden
brown. Transfer to a plate and
keep warm.
5 Cover the rice with water and
bring to the boil quickly. Remove
from the heat and pour off the
water.
6 Add the chicken, chicken stock
and tomatoes to the rice and
cook for about 10 minutes over a
low heat.
7 Add the peas and stir in. Cook
for a further 30–35 minutes over a
low heat, stirring occasionally.

CURRIED CHICKEN
Serves 4

2 medium onions, chopped
110g (4oz) margarine
57ml (2floz) oil
2 tbsp curry powder
2 dsp tomato purée
40g (1½oz) plain flour
575ml (1pt) chicken stock
1 tsp mixed spice
2 tsp chilli powder
2 tsp black pepper
2 tsp salt
4 chicken pieces, skinned and
    boned

METHOD 1 Sweat the onions in a small amount of margarine and oil.
2 Mix in and cook the tomato purée and flour, to make a 'roux' for the sauce. Add stock slowly and cook till thickened. Stir in the spices.
3 Skin and bone the chicken and fry in the margarine and oil for 10 minutes.
4 Add the chicken to the curry sauce and cook over a moderate heat for 15–20 minutes.
5 Serve on a bed of rice and gungo peas.

'Greedy choke puppy.'

CHICKEN 'PUPA-LICKIE'
Serves 6–8

Turning 'pupa-lickie' means doing a forward roll, and you just might do one when you have cooked this tasty dish!

1 tsp garlic powder or 1 clove
    garlic, chopped
2 tsp paprika
2 tsp salt
1 tsp black pepper
1 tsp thyme
50g (2oz) plain flour
6–8 chicken pieces

For the batter
110g (4oz) plain flour
275ml (½pt) milk
1 egg
2 tsp baking powder
1 dsp parsley
2 tsp salt
½ large can sweetcorn
deep fat or oil for frying

METHOD 1 Put all the dry ingredients into a bowl. Coat the chicken pieces with the mixture.
2 Place the chicken in a pressure cooker, just cover with water. Bring to pressure and cook for 10 minutes.
3 Reduce pressure and remove the chicken.
4 To make the batter, blend the flour, milk, egg, baking powder, parsley and salt. Beat well until smooth. Add the sweetcorn and mix well in.
5 Dip the chicken pieces into the batter, coating well. Fry in deep fat for 10 minutes. Drain and serve.

CHICKEN IN PINEAPPLE
Serves 4

28ml (1oz) vegetable oil
675g (1½lb) cooked, diced chicken
1 medium onion, chopped
1 tsp black pepper
1 tsp salt
1 tbsp curry powder
2 medium tomatoes, chopped
575ml (1pt) chicken stock or
    water
2 medium pineapples
25g (1oz) plain flour
25g (1oz) butter
parsley and sweet pepper rings
    for garnish

METHOD 1 Melt vegetable oil
and add the chicken,
chopped onion, pepper, salt,
curry powder and chopped
tomatoes. Cook for about 10-15
minutes.
2 Add the stock and cook for a
further 10 minutes.
3 Cut each pineapple in half,
lengthways. Cut out the flesh,
leaving an empty shell. Dice the
flesh.
4 Blend the flour and butter and
add gradually to pan. Stir until
smooth.
5 Add pineapple pieces and cook
for a further 6 minutes.
6 Grill the pineapple 'shell'.
7 Pour the chicken mixture into
the pineapple shell. Garnish
with parsley and pepper rings.
Serve with rice or salad.

GINGERY CHICKEN
Serves 4

4 chicken breasts
1 tsp saffron
25g (1oz) root ginger, peeled and
    grated
grated rind and juice of 2 limes or
    lemons
2 tsp chilli powder
2 tsp sugar
2 tsp salt
2 cloves garlic, crushed
3 medium onions, chopped
425ml ($\frac{3}{4}$pt) milk
275ml ($\frac{1}{2}$pt) coconut milk
    (see recipe in Puddings
    and Sweets)
25g (1oz) cornflour

METHOD 1 Put the chicken
breasts in a deep,
ovenproof dish. Season with
saffron and ginger. Add the juice
and rind of the limes or lemons.
2 Add the chilli powder, sugar,
salt, garlic and onions. Mix well
together so that the chicken is
well coated. Allow to stand.
3 Bring to the boil the milk and
coconut. Pour into a sieve and
squeeze with the back of a
wooden spoon, to render all the
'juice.' Discard the coconut
pieces, keeping some for garnish.
4 Pour the coconut milk over the
chicken mixture, cover with a lid
or foil and bake at 190°C (375°F)
Reg 5 for 40–45 minutes.
5 Mix the flour with a little water
and stir into the mixture during
the last 15 minutes of cooking
time.
6 Sprinkle with coconut before
serving.

SWEET POTATO STUFFING FOR CHICKEN OR TURKEY

Serves 6

Quantities are for a chicken; use double for a turkey.

275g (10oz) sausage meat
450g (1lb) sweet potatoes,
    cooked and mashed
2 medium onions, chopped
275g (10oz) soft white
    breadcrumbs
2 tsp grated nutmeg
2 cloves
1tsp thyme
salt and pepper

METHOD 1 Cook the sausage meat for 10 minutes over a low heat.
2 Add the cooked, mashed sweet potato together with the other ingredients and mix in well.
3 Cook for a further 3-5 minutes.
Cool and remove cloves before using.

Note As sweet potato becomes hard when cold, always reheat before use or have them freshly cooked and mashed.

Poultry

CARIBBEAN DUCK
Serves 2

1 medium onion
110g (4oz) butter
$\frac{1}{2}$ small red, $\frac{1}{2}$ small green sweet
    pepper chopped
110g (4oz) dried apricots
2 tbsp tomato purée
450g (1lb) long-grain rice, boiled
salt and black pepper
1 duck (or chicken if preferred),
    roasted
sweet pepper rings and parsley to
    garnish

For the sauce
110g (4oz) apricots
225ml (8fl oz) water
75g (3oz) brown sugar
2 dsp cornflour
rum to taste

METHOD 1 Sweat the onion in the butter. Add the chopped peppers, apricots and tomato purée. Cook until tender, about 10–12 minutes. Add the boiled rice. Stir in and season.
2 Take the roast duck (or chicken), split lengthways and remove bones.
3 Stuff with the rice and pepper mixture and keep warm.
4 To make the sauce, liquidize the apricots in a blender, put in a pan with the water and brown sugar. Bring to the boil, thicken with the cornflour and add the rum to taste.
5 Spoon the sauce over the duck before serving.
6 Garnish with sweet pepper rings and parsley.

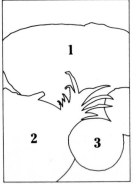

1 Caribbean Duck **2** Chicken Montego Bay **3** Chicken 'Run-Dun' (Run-Down)

CHICKEN MONTEGO BAY
Serves 4

4 chicken pieces
salt and pepper to taste
1 large pineapple
175g (6oz) brown sugar
175g (6oz) clear thin honey
25g (1oz) cornflour
110g (4oz) tomato purée
1 tsp thyme
1 tsp season-salt
1 tsp paprika
1 medium red and 1 medium green
   pepper, de-seeded and diced
chopped parsley for garnish

METHOD 1 Sprinkle the
chicken with salt and
pepper, and roast for 45 minutes
at 180°C (350°F) Reg 4.
2 Cut the pineapple into four,
lengthways. Remove the core and
a little flesh. Slice away from the
skin and cut into 12 segments,
then bake with the chicken for 15
minutes.
3 Transfer pulp and chicken
juices to a pan. Make up to 575ml
(1pt) with water. Add sugar,
honey, cornflour dissolved in a
little water, tomato purée and
seasonings.
4 Bring to the boil, then cook for
15 minutes or until well reduced.
Add pepper and heat through.
5 Arrange pineapple on a serving
dish. Top with chicken, sauce and
parsley.
See illustration on page 65

SALADS

Say the word 'salad' to the average woman and she will immediately think of lettuce, tomato and perhaps a little cucumber – if you are lucky!

Why be a dodo when there are so many wonderfully different fruits and vegetables about? You may not think of them straight away – in fact, you may never have used them before – but I'm sure that when you have tasted some of those I give in the recipes in this section, you will return to them again and again.

Remember what I said earlier, that 'You eat with your eyes first,' and that colour and presentation are very important, so be imaginative with the ingredients you choose. Experiment and create! Be a devil!

The decorations I have suggested need not be your choice, but remember to keep contrasting colours, shapes and textures in mind when you are thinking of, and preparing, garnishes. Serve your salads not just in large flat dishes but also in the shells and skins of the fruit and vegetables you use – coconuts, melons, pumpkins, grapefruit... As long as it's big and got enough curves, give it a try!

DUCK AND YAM SALAD
Serves 4-6

½ roast duck, diced
450g (1lb) yam, boiled for 10
    minutes then diced
110ml (4fl oz) salad cream
1 tsp cayenne pepper
1 tsp cinnamon
1 tsp nutmeg
salt and pepper to taste
orange slices, peppers and nuts
    for decoration

METHOD 1 Mix all the
    ingredients together,
then lay out on a serving plate or
dish, and decorate with the fruit
and nuts. (Chicken can be used
instead of duck.)

YAM SALAD
Serves 4

This is the Caribbean equivalent
of potato salad.

1 medium watermelon
450g (1lb) yams, boiled for 10-15
    minutes and cooled
4 tbsp salad cream
1 small onion, chopped
salt and pepper to taste
large prawns and avocado for
    decoration

METHOD 1 Cut the melon into
    a basket shape and
remove the pink flesh (keep it for
cocktails later!).
2 Cut the yam into large cubes,
mix with the other ingredients,
and pile into the melon skin.
3 Decorate with large prawns and
strips of avocado. Do this just
before serving, or the avocado
will discolour.

PLANTAIN SALAD
Serves 2

2 ripe yellow plantains
oil for frying
oranges, lime skin and melon for
    decoration

METHOD 1 Cut the plantains
    into quarters and skin.
2 Heat oil, and deep-fry for 6
minutes. Allow to cool.
3 Decorate as desired with the
fruit.

SWEET POTATO SALAD
Serves 2-3

450g (1lb) sweet potato
salt to taste
3 sprigs shallot, chopped
white pepper
75g (3oz) butter
mayonnaise to taste

METHOD 1 Peel the sweet
    potato and boil in
salted water for 15-20 minutes.
Drain as soon as possible.
2 Dice the potato in a bowl while
warm. Mix gently with the
chopped shallot, pepper, butter
and mayonnaise.

RED PEA AND SWEETCORN SALAD
Serves 6

225g (8oz) red peas (kidney
    beans)
salt and pepper to taste
2 cloves garlic, chopped
450g (1lb) white patna rice,
    boiled
175g (6oz) sweetcorn, cooked
1 onion, chopped
25g (1oz) ginger root, peeled
    and chopped

For the vinaigrette dressing
2 tbsp cider vinegar
salt and freshly ground black
    pepper to taste
6–8 tbsp sunflower oil
2 tbsp fresh garden herbs
    (chives, parsley, basil, etc)

1 Soak the peas
overnight in cold
water.
2 Next day, add the salt, pepper
and garlic and boil for 1 hour
until tender. Drain. (The liquid
can be used as a tasteful base for
soup.)
3 Mix all the ingredients together
in a salad bowl.
4 To make the dressing put all the
ingredients, except the herbs, into
a screw-top glass jar and shake
vigorously. Add the herbs just
before using.

Note As this salad is made from
cooked ingredients, it should be
made well in advance so that the
vegetables can absorb the
dressing.

PUMPKIN AND CASHEW NUT SALAD
Serves 6–8

450g (1lb) pumpkin, boiled for
    10 minutes and cooled
110g (4oz) cashew nuts
4 tbsp vinaigrette (oil and vinegar
    dressing)
salt and pepper
slices of watermelon and green
    pepper for decoration

METHOD 1 Cube the cooked
pumpkin and mix with
the other ingredients.
2 Decorate with the melon and
peppers.
See illustration on page 73

COCO AND CHOW-CHOW SALAD
Serves 4

1 medium chow-chow (similar to
    marrow), peeled, seeded
    and boiled for 10 minutes in
    salted water
450g (1lb) coco (similar to
    potato), peeled and boiled
    together with the chow-
    chow
5 tbsp salad cream
110g (4oz) pistachio nuts,
    shelled
salt and pepper
chopped chives, orange slices,
    grapes and tomatoes for
    decoration

METHOD 1 Roughly chop the
chow-chow and coco
and mix with the other
ingredients.
2 Lay them on a serving dish and
decorate.
See illustration on page 73

AVOCADO AND CHICKEN
SALAD WITH CREAM DRESSING
Serves 4

3 ripe avocados
juice of $\frac{1}{2}$ lemon
salt to taste
2 tbsp chives, chopped
1 clove garlic, chopped
225g (8oz) chicken, diced
paprika for garnish

For the cream dressing
1 small onion, chopped
salt and pepper to taste
1 tbsp Dijon mustard
1 tsp parsley, chopped
2 tbsp lemon or lime juice
6 tbsp double cream

METHOD 1 Peel and stone the avocados.
2 Cut the flesh into cubes. Sprinkle with lemon juice, salt, chives and garlic.
3 Gently stir in the diced chicken.
4 To make the cream dressing, mix the onion, salt, pepper, mustard and parsley together.
5 Bind with the lemon or lime juice, then add the fresh double cream and beat together.
6 Pour over the salad or serve separately. Sprinkle with paprika.

VEGETABLE DISHES

FRIED YAM CAKES
Makes about 30 cakes

675g (1½lb) fresh yams (or sweet
    potato)
25g (1oz) butter, melted and
    cooled
1 small onion, finely grated
2 tbsp fresh parsley, finely
    chopped
2 tsp salt
2 tsp black pepper
3 egg yolks
4 tbsp vegetable oil

METHOD 1 Boil the yams or
sweet potato for about
25 minutes until tender.
2 Pour away the water and mash
in a deep bowl with the butter,
onions, parsley, salt and pepper;
mix well.
3 Drop in the egg yolks, one at a
time, and beat well until the
mixture is fairly smooth (or use a
food mixer to combine the
ingredients).
4 Heat the oil in a large heavy
pan. Drop tablespoonfuls of the
yam mixture into the oil and
cook, 4-5 at a time, leaving room
for them to spread, for about 5
minutes each side until golden
and crisp.
5 Drain on kitchen paper and
serve at once.

TROPICAL VEGETABLE PIE
Serves 4

In the Caribbean this would
usually be an economy dish, but
in Britain it makes a nice
vegetarian alternative which you
can also serve alongside meat.

1 small chow-chow
1 small coco
110g (4oz) pumpkin
225g (8oz) yam
1 small tin tomatoes
1 small onion, chopped
salt and black pepper

For the white sauce
25g (1oz) butter
25g (1oz) flour
275ml (½pt) milk

For the topping
50-110g (2-4oz) grated cheese

METHOD 1 Peel and rinse the
chow-chow, coco,
pumpkin and yam. Cut in half
(removing the chow-chow
kernel) and boil for 10 minutes.
2 Drain off water, allow to cool,
then chop into slices.
3 Place sliced vegetables in a pie-
dish in layers.
4 Mix the canned tomatoes with
the chopped onion, season with
salt and pepper and pour over the
vegetables.
5 Mix the ingredients for the white
sauce and pour over. Sprinkle
with the grated cheese topping
and bake for about 15 minutes at
180°C (350°F) Reg 4.

'Bit-bit mek poun'.
(Proverb)

FREEDOM EGGS
Serves 3

2 small onions, very thinly sliced
1 medium tomato, very thinly sliced
75g (3oz) butter
40g (1½oz) plain flour
275ml (½pt) milk
pinch of grated nutmeg
6 hard-boiled eggs, chopped
salt and pepper to taste
parsley for garnish

METHOD 1 Gently fry the
onion and tomato in
25g (1oz) butter for 5 minutes.
2 Mix the rest of the butter and
flour together as in a roux. Gently
add small amounts of the flour-
butter mixture to the milk in a
saucepan.
3 Bring the mixture to the boil
over a medium heat, stirring
continuously until it thickens
(about 10 minutes). Remove
from the heat.
4 Add all the other ingredients,
mixing in carefully.
5 Serve hot or cold in individual
dishes with coco bread. Garnish
with parsley

STUFFED EGGS
Serves 3

6 eggs, hard-boiled
2 sprigs parsley
50g (2oz) celery, finely chopped
1 tsp salt
1 tsp pepper
2 tsp vinegar
3 tbsp mayonnaise
50g (2oz) minced ham
paprika and extra parsley for
garnish

METHOD 1 Cut the eggs in
half length ways and
scoop out the yolks.
2 Keeping the whites, place the
yolks together with all the other
ingredients in a liquidizer.
3 Liquidize until smooth. Pipe the
filling back into the egg halves.
4 Sprinkle with paprika and
garnish with parsley.

1 Pumpkin and Cashew Nut Salad
2 Coco and Chow-Chow Salad

Vegetable Dishes

RICE AND GUNGO PEAS
Serves 6

This is the traditional accompaniment to Ackee and Saltfish (see Fish recipes).

225g (8oz) gungo peas or red kidney beans, soaked overnight
1 tsp thyme, chopped
25g (1oz) butter
50g (2oz) coconut cream
salt and black pepper to taste
1 chilli, de-seeded and chopped
2 tbsp shallot or spring onion, chopped finely
1.1–1.4l (2–2½pt) water
450g (1lb) long-grain rice

METHOD 1 Put gungo peas or red kidney beans into a pan. Add the thyme, butter and coconut cream. Season to taste. Cover with water, bring to the boil and cook for ¾–1 hour, until soft to the touch.
2 Add the rice, and more water if needed, and cook for a further 25–30 minutes over a very low heat.

RUSTIE'S VEGETARIAN CALYPSO
Serves 2

1 pineapple
110g (4oz) yam
110g (4oz) coco
1 chow-chow
110g (4oz) pumpkin
1×425g (15oz) tin ackee
slices of red and green peppers for garnish

For the sauce
2 dsp tomato purée
275ml (½pt) water
salt and pepper to taste

METHOD 1 Cut the pineapple lengthways and scoop out the flesh. Peel and chop the vegetables.
2 Cook all the vegetables together (yam, coco and chow-chow) for about 15 minutes, adding the pumpkin last. When tender, drain.
3 To make the sauce, mix the tomato purée in the water and season to taste.
4 Mash the vegetables, pour over the sauce and mix together. Add the ackee and pineapple and stir in well.
5 Put the mixture back into the pineapple 'shell', garnish with slices of red and green peppers and serve with rice.

STUFFED PEPPERS, VEGETARIAN STYLE, WITH OKRAS
Serves 4

110g (4oz) Protaveg (soya, beef
    flavour)
25g (1oz) coconut cream
salt and pepper to taste
1.1l (2pt) water, of which 275ml
    ($\frac{1}{2}$pt) to cook okras,
    remainder to pour over
    peppers
8 large sweet peppers
450g (1lb) long-grain rice,
    cooked
1 tsp rosemary
1 tsp chilli powder
1 tsp thyme
$\frac{1}{2}$ medium onion, chopped
2 medium tomatoes, chopped
225g (8oz) okras
2 tsp tomato purée

METHOD 1 Boil the Protaveg,
    coconut cream, salt
and pepper in about 850ml (1$\frac{1}{2}$pt)
water for 10–15 minutes. Drain
and keep the juice.
2 Cut the tops off the peppers,
remove the seeds and pith, and
set aside.
3 Mix the rice, rosemary, chilli
powder, thyme, onion, tomatoes
and Protaveg together and stuff
the peppers, filling to the top.
4 Stand the peppers in an
ovenproof, high-sided dish, pour
the drained juice from the
Protaveg over, replace the tops on
the peppers, and bake for 35–40
minutes at 160°C (325°F) Reg 3.
5 Wearing rubber gloves, cut the
tops from the okras and wash
thoroughly in a sieve.
6 Mix the tomato purée with
about 275ml ($\frac{1}{2}$pt) water in a
saucepan. Add the okras, bring to
the boil and cook for 10–15
minutes until tender but not
mushy. Serve as the vegetable
accompaniment to the peppers.

SWEET POTATO PIE CRUST
Serves 4

As a change from short-crust
pastry, why not try using sweet
potato in the mixture? You will be
amazed at the taste! Make sure
you use the Boniato sweet potato,
which is now widely available in
Britain. It has a brown or pink
skin and white flesh. (The yellow-
fleshed variety is too sweet and
too moist, so avoid it.)

110g (4oz) sweet potato
225g (8oz) plain flour
1 tsp salt
110g (4oz) butter
2 tsp baking powder
150ml ($\frac{1}{4}$pt) water to bind

METHOD 1 Boil and mash the
    sweet potato.
2 Rub together flour, salt, butter
and baking powder.
3 Gently mix in the mashed sweet
potatoes with a spoon.
4 Bind together with the water to
make a dough. Allow to stand in
the refrigerator for 10–15 minutes.
5 On a floured board, roll the
dough out into the required
shape.
6 Bake in a hot oven at 200°C
(400°F) Reg 6 for 20–25 minutes.

**'What a man doan know, older
dan him.'**

EGGPLANT CREOLE
Serves 4

Eggplant is another name for aubergine, now widely available in the shops. Try this recipe for a really great supper dish.

2 medium eggplants
3 tbsp butter
1×425g (15oz) tin tomatoes
3 tbsp plain flour
1 medium green sweet pepper, de-seeded and chopped
1 small onion, chopped
1 tsp salt
1 tbsp brown sugar
½ bay leaf
2 cloves of garlic (optional)
50g (2oz) white breadcrumbs and 50g (2oz) grated cheese for topping.

 **METHOD** 1 Peel the eggplants and cut into small pieces. Cool in a small amount of water.
2 Drain and place in a greased dish.
3 Melt the butter. Add the tomatoes, flour and all the other ingredients.
4 Cook for 5 minutes over a medium heat, stirring continuously.
5 Pour the mixture over the eggplants, sprinkle with the breadcrumbs and grated cheese. Bake in a moderate oven at 180°C (350°F) Reg 4 for 30 minutes.

'Me feel it to me soul-case, for
Me know wha' mek dem fall.
Dem bwoy naw pay attention to
Dem duckanoo an' saal!'
(From *Six Nil*, by Louise Bennett)

DUCKANOO
Serves 8

Here is a traditional dish which originated in Africa and came to the Islands with the slaves. It uses the 'parcel' method of cooking and is always steamed.

900g (2lb) sweet potato, grated
1 small coconut, grated
225g (8oz) sugar
2 tsp vanilla essence
1 tsp salt
2 tsp nutmeg
175g (6oz) margarine
175g (6oz) plain flour
milk to mix
8 × 20cm (8in) squares of cooking foil

METHOD 1 Mix all the ingredients together thoroughly. Bind with the milk to a 'dropping' consistency.
2 Place 2 large spoonfuls of the mixture into the foil squares. Fold into parcels and seal the edges with the fingers.
3 Steam in a pressure cooker for 35–40 minutes. Alternatively, bake in the oven at 190°C (375°F) Reg 5 for 40–45 minutes.

1 Eggplant Creole **2** Duckanoo

SWEET POTATO PIE
Serves 4

450g (1lb) sweet potatoes
110g (4oz) margarine
175g (6oz) soft brown sugar
2 eggs
2 tsp caramel colouring
225g (8oz) plain flour
1 tsp cinnamon
2 tsp nutmeg
110g (4oz) sultanas
175ml (6fl oz) milk

 1 Peel potatoes and boil for 10–15 minutes. Mash.
2 Cream the margarine and sugar. Add the eggs gradually until the mixture is fluffy. Add the caramel colouring and mix in thoroughly.
3 Mix together all the dry ingredients apart from the sultanas. Add to the creamed mixture.
4 Add the sultanas, then the milk, stirring until smooth.
5 Grease a 20cm (8in) pie-dish. Put mixture into dish and bake for 40 minutes at 180°C (350°F) Reg 4.

'Sweet sweet potato pie,
One for the doctor, two for the maid,
Three for the little baby...'

CONKIES
Serves 6-8

Traditionally, these are served on Guy Fawkes Day, but as for the origin of the custom and what the word means, no-one seems to know! The mixture should really be cooked wrapped in banana leaves, so, unless you happen to have a banana tree growing in the back garden, you will have to manage with cooking foil!

Conkies are a real knock-out!

175g (6oz) grated coconut
110g (4oz) pumpkin, peeled and grated
225g (8oz) sweet potatoes
175g (6oz) brown sugar
2 tsp allspice
2 tsp nutmeg
2 tsp almond essence
175g (6oz) stoned raisins
75g (3oz) plain flour
225g (8oz) cornmeal
175g (6oz) butter, melted
275ml ($\frac{1}{2}$pt) milk
20cm (8in) squares of cooking foil to make the parcels

METHOD 1 In a deep bowl, combine all the ingredients. Mix together until a smooth paste is achieved.
2 Spread the squares of cooking foil out flat on a table and with a large spoon put 2–3 spoonfuls into the centre of the foil.
3 Fold over into a parcel shape and seal the edges with the fingers.
4 Steam in a pressure cooker for 30 minutes or in a steamer over a pan of boiling water for 1 hour.

STUFFED POTATOES
Serves 12

12 medium-sized potatoes
oil for frying
2 large onions
450g (1lb) minced beef
2 beef stock cubes
425ml (¾pt) water
salt and pepper to taste
4 tbsp tomato purée

 1 Peel potatoes and
cut across the top.
Scoop out centre.
2 Deep-fry potatoes until light
brown. Remove from heat and
drain off oil.
3 Fry onions and then add the
mince. Dissolve 1 stock cube in
275ml (½pt) water and pour over
the mince and onions. Add salt
and pepper and cook for 10
minutes.
4 Add tomato purée and cook for
a further 10 minutes. The mixture
should be nice and thick. Allow to
cool.
5 Using a teaspoon, stuff potatoes
with the mixture.
6 Take the scooped-out potato
flesh and line a pie-dish. Arrange
the stuffed potatoes on top.
7 Dissolve the other stock cube in
the remaining water and pour
over potatoes. Cook for 20–25
minutes at 190°C (375°F) Reg 5.
Serve with rice and green salad.

SPAGHETTI A LA SPIKE
Serves 4

I created this dish especially for
Spike Milligan, who is a
vegetarian and very fond of
spaghetti. 'In the Catford Islands,'
he told me, 'it grows on trees!'

450g (1lb) spaghetti
water for boiling

For the sauce
1 tbsp olive oil
25g (1oz) butter
2 cloves garlic, chopped
1 medium onion, chopped
1 dsp parsley, fresh or dried
1 tsp basil
450g (1lb) fresh tomatoes,
de-seeded and chopped
2 tsp black pepper
2 tsp salt
110g (4oz) Parmesan cheese

METHOD 1 Boil spaghetti in
enough water to cover,
for 10–15 minutes. Drain to keep
warm.
2 To make the sauce, heat the oil
and butter, add the garlic and
cook. Add the onions and brown
slightly.
3 Add the parsley, basil, chopped
tomatoes, black pepper and salt.
Stir in well and cook over a
medium heat for 10 minutes.
4 Pour the sauce over the
spaghetti and sprinkle with
Parmesan cheese.

SAVOURY CABBAGE
Serves 6-8

Do you have trouble getting the family to eat cabbage? Then try cooking it this way. I guarantee you will have them shouting for more!

1 large firm white cabbage
1.5l (3pt) hot water
1 tsp each of salt and pepper

For the stuffing
225g (8oz) white, washed Patna rice
450g (1lb) minced beef
225g (8oz) onion, chopped or liquidized
1 bunch parsley, chopped or liquidized
110g (4oz) margarine
2 tsp salt
2 tsp black pepper
2 dsp tomato purée
4 tsp dried mint
2 dsp vegetable oil

For the sauce
275ml (½pt) hot water
2 dsp tomato purée
1 beef stock cube

METHOD 1 Take off the coarse outer leaves and wash the cabbage. Place in a saucepan containing 1.5l (3pt) water, salt and pepper. Boil for 10 minutes.
2 Remove as many leaves as will come away easily. Place the cabbage back in the saucepan and repeat the process until you reach the heart.
3 Slice the heart and lay at the bottom of the saucepan to form a bed. Put leaves back into the water and cook for 2-3 minutes to soften.
4 Cut away central stems, then cut leaves in half.
5 Mix all the ingredients for the stuffing together and place 1 dessertspoon on each leaf. Roll up into a parcel, sealing the ends with the fingers.
6 Place the parcels on the bed of cabbage. Mix the ingredients for the sauce and pour over. Cook for 35-40 minutes on a low heat.

CRUNCHY PUMPKIN AND YAM PIE
Serves 6-8

675g (1½lb) pumpkin, peeled, de-seeded and chopped
900g (2lb) yam, peeled and chopped
water to boil
2 tsp paprika
2 tsp chilli powder
1 tbsp parsley
2 tsp black pepper
2 tsp thyme
50g (2oz) flaked almonds
1 tbsp salt (for cooking)
Nutty Crunch cornflakes for topping
50g (2oz) butter

METHOD 1 Boil and mash down the pumpkin and yam. Drain.
2 Add the paprika, chilli powder, parsley, black pepper, thyme and flaked almonds.
3 Put the mixture into an ovenproof dish. Add salt and top with the cornflakes and knobs of butter. Cover with foil.
4 Bake at 190°C (375°F) Reg 5 for 15-20 minutes.

COCO FRITTERS

Serves 4

900g (2lb) coco
6 tbsp water or enough to bind
50g (2oz) plain flour
1 medium onion, grated
salt and pepper to taste
a few chives, chopped
2 egg whites, whisked
oil for frying
parsley for garnish

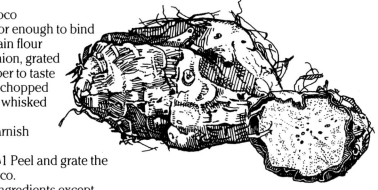

METHOD 1 Peel and grate the coco.
2 Put all the ingredients except the egg whites into a deep bowl. Add the water and beat together.
3 Fold in the beaten egg white carefully.
4 Heat the oil and drop spoonfuls of the mixture into it. Fry till golden.
5 Drain on kitchen paper. Serve garnished with parsley.

SAVOURY DUMPLIN'S

Serves 4

Here is what you need to add that 'greatness' to stews and casseroles!

3 tbsp margarine
110g (4oz) plain flour
pinch of salt
1 tsp baking powder
1 tsp chopped onion
1 tsp chopped chives
1 tsp chopped parsley
water to bind

'Sarah, you see nobody pass here?
No, me frien'.
Well, one o' me dumplins gone!'
(Traditional song)

METHOD 1 Rub the margarine and flour together in a deep bowl.
2 Add all the other ingredients and bind together with enough water to make a stiff dough.
3 Knead lightly and form into balls. Add to stews or casseroles and cook for 30 minutes.

ACKEE SOUFFLÉ
Serves 4-6

40g (1½oz) butter
4 tbsp plain flour
150ml (¼pt) milk
1 tsp salt
1 tsp white pepper
1 dsp Worcestershire sauce
4 eggs, separated
1×425g (15oz) tin ackee,
    mashed to a purée

METHOD 1 Melt the butter in a pan. Stir in the flour carefully and cook for 1 minute. Do not allow flour to brown!
2 Heat the milk and add all at once to the flour mixture. Stir over a medium heat until thick and smooth.
3 Add the salt and pepper and Worcestershire sauce. Stir in well.
4 Remove from the heat and cool.
5 Separate the eggs and stir the yolks into the mixture gently, then stir in the ackee purée. Beat the whites until they 'peak'.
6 Take a small amount of the beaten egg whites and mix in. Fold in the rest.
7 Pour the mixture into a deep soufflé dish and bake for about 30 minutes at 190°C (375°F) Reg 5. Serve immediately.

CORNBAKE
Serves 6

If 'bake' suggests an American dish, as in Clam Bake, it is also a word used in the Caribbean. In Trinidad, for instance, they call Fried Dumplin' a 'Bake'.

2 eggs
25g (1oz) butter
75g (3oz) cornmeal
1 small can sweetcorn
1 can evaporated milk, small
1 medium onion, chopped
salt and pepper
½ medium green sweet pepper,
    de-seeded and chopped

METHOD 1 In a blender, combine all the ingredients except the sweet pepper.
2 Liquidize until smooth. Put into a bowl, add the green pepper and mix well.
3 Turn into a greased baking dish and bake at 150°C (300°F) Reg 2 until set – about 30-40 minutes.

PUDDINGS AND SWEETS

BEWDLEY STRAWBERRY FLAN
Serves 6–8

This beautiful old town on the banks of the River Severn, in Worcestershire, is where I live. Some of the most delicious strawberries that I have ever tasted are grown in the area, so I created this flan in celebration of those mouth-watering delights!

1 pkt gelatine or jelly glaze
2 tbsp redcurrant jelly
1 flan case, home-made or bought
675g (1½lb) strawberries (1 punnet per person)
110ml (4 fl oz) vodka
275ml (½pt) whipping cream
25g (1oz) almonds, flaked and toasted
25g (1oz) chocolate

METHOD 1 Make up the jelly glaze or gelatine as instructed on the pack. Stir in the redcurrant jelly.
2 Seal the base of the flan case with the gelatine or jelly mixture.
3 Clean and wash the strawberries. Drain and cover the base with them, packing well.
4 Pour over the vodka and leave to soak in.
5 Whip the cream and, using a large star nozzle, pipe it round the edge of the case and over the fruit.
6 Decorate with the flaked almonds. Melt the chocolate over a pan of hot water, put into a small piping bag and 'drizzle' over the flan.

JAMAICA PUMPKIN PIE
Serves 6–8

175g (6oz) short-crust pastry
450g (1lb) pumpkin, steamed or stewed
225g (8oz) sugar
½ tsp salt
½ tsp ginger
1 tsp cinnamon
½ tsp allspice
2 eggs, beaten

METHOD 1 Roll out the pastry and line a 20cm (8in) sponge tin. Prick all over the base with a fork.
2 Mix the pumpkin, sugar, salt, ginger, cinnamon and allspice together in a bowl. Beat well.
3 Add the beaten eggs and beat for 2 minutes.
4 Pour into the pastry case, and place in a hot oven at 200°C (400°F) Reg 6. Reduce the heat to 180°C (350°F) Reg 4 after 15 minutes.
5 Continue to bake for 45 minutes, when the pastry should be golden brown and the pumpkin custard set and uncurdled.

STUFFED BANANA SUPREME
Serves 4

110g (4oz) butter
110g (4oz) icing sugar
110g (4oz) seedless raisins
4 tbsp dark rum
4 very large bananas, nicely
    ripened
3 tbsp lemon juice
50g (2oz) toasted almonds
8 glacé cherries
57ml (2floz) double cream,
    whipped

METHOD 1 Cream the butter
and sugar together.
2 Put the raisins to soak in half
the rum.
3 Wash, top and tail bananas, and
split the skin lengthways. Open
each out into a V shape and place
in a serving dish. Sprinkle with
lemon juice.
4 Beat the remaining rum into the
butter-sugar mixture and stir in
the raisins.
5 Spoon the mixture into the
hollow in the bananas. Decorate
with the almonds, cherries, and
whipped cream.

RUSTIES PASHKA
Serves 6-8

Pashka is a traditional Russian
pudding of curd cheese, spices,
dried fruits and sugar, eaten at
Easter to celebrate the end of
Lent. I made this version in
honour of that fine actor, Peter
Ustinov, who joined me in the
kitchen at TV-am.
    It is a very rich pudding, yet
light and absolutely delicious!

5 large egg yolks
450g (1lb) caster sugar
275ml ($\frac{1}{2}$pt) milk
225g (8oz) unsalted butter
1.6kg (3$\frac{1}{2}$lb) curd cheese
275ml ($\frac{1}{2}$pt) fresh double cream,
    whipped
2 tsp vanilla essence
1 tbsp currants (optional)
50g (2oz) almonds, finely
    chopped
75g (3oz) mixed peel
zest of 1 lemon
1 sachet gelatine (made up as per
    instructions on pack)

METHOD 1 Cream together
the egg yolks and
sugar. Stir in the milk.
2 Put this mixture into a double
boiler and bring to the boil slowly.
Add the butter.
3 Add the mixture to the curd
cheese in a deep bowl.
4 Stir in the fresh cream, and the
vanilla essence. Add the currants,
almonds, mixed peel and lemon
zest. Stir in the gelatine.
5 Line a basin with a large square
of muslin and fill with the
mixture.
6 Fold over the ends and place in
the refrigerator to set for 2-3
hours.
7 To serve, turn out onto a plate
or serving dish. Decorate with
whipping cream and almonds.

BARBECUED BANANAS
Serves 1

2-3 bananas (firm, not over-ripe)
57ml (2floz) dark rum, banana
    liqueur or coconut liqueur
2 dsp brown sugar
1 tbsp nutmeg
juice of 1 large lemon
25g (1oz) sultanas
110ml (4 floz) whipped cream

METHOD 1 Wash, top and tail the fruit. Slit the skins down one side. Grill for 5-6 minutes at full heat, or microwave for 3 minutes, until the skins are charred and the bananas are soft.
2 Open the skins out, sprinkle with rum, banana liqueur or coconut liqueur, brown sugar, nutmeg, lemon juice and sultanas.
3 Pipe with fresh cream.
4 Eat with a spoon from the skin.

RUSTIE'S BANANA FRITTERS
Serves 2

I have two variations which I use. Why not try them both, for they are really super!

50g (2oz) plain flour
pinch of salt
2 egg whites
4 tbsp milk
2-3 large bananas
oil for frying

METHOD 1 Sift the flour and salt into a deep bowl, add the salt and beat in the milk a little at a time. Set aside for 20-30 minutes.
2 Whisk the egg whites until stiff and fold into the batter.
3 Peel the bananas, cut in half lengthways and then into 2 or 3 across.

4 Coat each piece of banana with the batter and fry in smoking hot oil until golden brown.
5. Drain on kitchen paper, sprinkle with sugar and serve very hot.

———

OR

———

225g (8oz) self-raising flour
1 egg
275ml ($\frac{1}{2}$pt) milk
5-6 large ripe bananas, mashed
110g (4oz) sugar
1 tsp nutmeg
1 tsp vanilla essence
oil for frying

METHOD 1 Sift the flour into a deep bowl. Make a well in the centre and add the egg. Beat gently into the flour, add the milk, a little at a time, to make a smooth batter.
2 Add the mashed bananas, sugar and spices. Beat in well. Leave to rest for 10 minutes in the refrigerator.
3. Heat the oil. Drop in spoonfuls of the mixture and fry for about 6-8 minutes on each side. Serve at once. It's delicious with ice cream.
See illustration on page 97

BANANA TOASTIES
Serves 5

For a quick sweet, nothing could
be easier or more tasty than this!

3 eggs, beaten
150ml (5fl oz) milk
10 slices bread, crusts removed
75g (3oz) butter
4 large bananas, peeled and
        thinly sliced
3 tsp strained lemon juice
3 tbsp brown sugar
6 tbsp rum

METHOD 1 Combine the eggs
and milk in a large flat
dish. Dip in bread and coat both
sides.
2 Heat the butter and fry each
slice until golden.
3 Drain, and cover one side with
sliced banana. Sprinkle with
lemon juice and cover with
another slice of bread. Sprinkle
with sugar and cut each banana
toastie diagonally.
4 Pour over a little rum and, if you
fancy it, serve with whipped
cream and flaked chocolate
topped with a slice of banana!

PLANTAIN CRISPS
Serves 2

2 ripe plantains
flour and cinnamon for dusting
50g (2oz) butter or margarine

METHOD 1 Slice the plantains
into convenient-sized
rounds or strips.
2 Dust with the flour and
cinnamon.
3 Heat the butter and fry the
plantains quickly until golden.
Drain on kitchen paper.
4 Serve hot or cold with drinks.

Note Plantains can also be used
as a vegetable by simply peeling,
cutting in halves, then into
quarters and frying in deep oil for
4-5 minutes. Delicious!

PINEAPPLE AND MANGO PIE
Serves 6

You will need a 30cm (12in) flan dish for this pie - and remember to keep the pineapple top for decoration.

For the pastry
450g (1lb) plain flour
225g (8oz) butter
110g (4oz) caster sugar
2 eggs

For the filling
1 large fresh pineapple
1 large mango, peeled and sliced
110g (4oz) caster sugar
1 tsp cinnamon
1 tsp vanilla essence
275ml ($\frac{1}{2}$pt) water
$1\frac{1}{2}$ dsp cornflour
50g (2oz) icing sugar for dusting

METHOD 1 To make the pastry, sieve the flour into a deep bowl and rub in the butter. Add the sugar and rub this in.
2 Add the eggs and mould together into a dough. Take half the pastry, roll out and line the flan dish.
3 Bake 'blind' (with greaseproof paper in the centre containing beans or breadcrusts) for 10 minutes at 190°C (375°F) Reg 5. Remove from the oven.
4 To make the filling, peel and core the pineapple and dice. Peel and slice the mango lengthways. Remove the stone and chop roughly.
5 Cook the pineapple, mango, sugar, spice, vanilla essence and water, together with the cornflour dissolved in a little of the water, for 5 minutes.
6 Put the mixture into the flan case. Roll out the rest of the pastry to make a lid. Cover the flan, cut slits in the lid and bake for 20-25 minutes at 190°C (375°F) Reg 5.
7 Allow to cool. Decorate with the pineapple top by cutting a hole in the centre of the pie, and placing the pineapple top into it. Dust with the icing sugar.
See illustration on page 101

DRUNKEN PINEAPPLE
Serves 3

Guaranteed to make you light-headed!

1 small ripe pineapple
rum to taste
3 tbsp brown sugar

METHOD 1 Do not remove the leaves from the fruit!
2 Cut the pineapple into 3 sections, lengthways, slicing through the leaves.
3 Cut the flesh from each 'shell' in one piece, using a sharp knife. Cut out the core.
4 Halve the flesh lengthways, then cut through crossways into bite-size pieces.
5 Put the 'shells' into individual dishes, replace the flesh in a 'staggered' fashion, then pour a generous amount of rum over.
6 Sprinkle with brown sugar and 'flash' under a hot grill. Serve immediately.

RUSTIE'S MOCHA MOUSSE
Serves 4

110g (4oz) butter
350g (12oz) caster sugar
4 eggs, separated
3 tbsp boiling water
1½ tbsp instant coffee powder or granules
275g (10oz) cocoa powder
225ml (8floz) double cream
4 tbsp Tia Maria

METHOD 1 In a deep bowl, beat the butter and sugar together until creamy.
2 Beat the egg yolks into the mixture gradually, until fluffy.
3 With the boiling water, dissolve the coffee and cocoa together. Set aside.
4 Beat the cream until thick. (Keep a little back for decoration.)
5 Whisk the egg whites until they 'peak'. Gently fold the egg whites and the fresh cream in the coffee-cocoa liquid using a metal spoon.
6 Now gently fold in the Tia Maria. Spoon the mixture into individual bowls. Pipe with fresh cream and chocolate curls. To make these, chill a bar of milk or plain chocolate in the refrigerator; when needed, shave off 'curls' from the bar with a vegetable peeler.

RUSTIE'S CHRISTMAS PUDDING

Serves 8

225g (8oz) beef suet, chopped
225g (8oz) stoned raisins
225g (8oz) sultanas
350g (12oz) currants
225g (8oz) mixed peel, chopped
225g (8oz) soft brown sugar
225g (8oz) breadcrumbs
75g (3oz) strong flour
20g ($\frac{3}{4}$oz) mixed spice
1 tsp salt
5 eggs
zest and juice of 2 lemons
zest and juice of 1 orange
sherry and rum to taste

METHOD 1 In a deep bowl, mix all the ingredients together and allow to stand for 48 hours.
2 Fill a buttered basin to the brim with the mixture. Cover with buttered greaseproof paper and tie down with a piece of muslin.
3 Steam for 4–6 hours, according to the size of your basin.

4 To serve, unmould on a round dish and decorate with a sprig of berried holly. Pour over some warming spirit (brandy or rum) and light just before bringing to the table.
See illustration on page 109

LIGHT COCONUT JELLY
Serves 4

Just watch the kids go for it!

575ml (1pt) milk
1 medium fresh coconut, grated
2 sachets gelatine
2 tbsp sugar

METHOD 1 Heat the milk and pour over the coconut. Leave to stand for about 10 minutes.
2 Stir, then squeeze through a fine sieve, pressing well to extract the full coconut flavour.
3 Reheat the milk, add the gelatine and the sugar. Stir until they dissolve.
4 Pour into a mould and leave until set.
5 To serve, turn out on a serving dish. Decorate with rosettes of whipped cream and glacé cherries.

'When cockroach gi' party, him no ax fowl.'

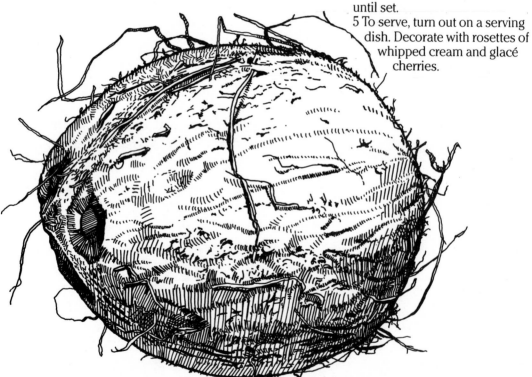

COCONUT MILK

1 coconut
275ml ($\frac{1}{2}$pt) water

METHOD 1 Pierce the 'fleshy' eye of the coconut and drain out the water. Strain.
2 Crack the coconut with a hammer on a hard surface and remove the 'meat' from the shell. Grate as finely as possible into a bowl.
3 Pour over 275ml ($\frac{1}{2}$pt) boiling water and allow to stand for 1 hour.
4 Caribbean ladies generally use their hands to squeeze the coconut, but if you would prefer, squeeze it through a very fine sieve with the back of a spoon.
5 For **Coconut Cream,** allow the coconut milk to stand until the cream rises to the top. It is thick, rich and absolutely superb with desserts!

Note Amounts vary with the freshness and quality of the coconut, but the average coconut weighs about 675g ($1\frac{1}{2}$lb) and yields between 225g (8oz) and 450g (1lb) of grated 'meat'.

RICH COCONUT PUDDING
Serves 4

1 large fresh coconut
1 large tin evaporated milk
$\frac{1}{2}$ tin condensed milk
3 tbsp white sugar
4 sachets gelatine
575ml (1pt) water

METHOD 1 Crack the coconut, scoop out the 'meat' and grate. Leaving some aside for decoration, put remainder into a muslin cloth or sieve over a large bowl.
2 Boil together 275ml ($\frac{1}{2}$pt) evaporated milk and 275ml ($\frac{1}{2}$pt) water. Pour over the grated coconut and leave to stand until cool.
3 Squeeze through the cloth or sieve.
4 Pour a further 275ml ($\frac{1}{2}$pt) water over the coconut and squeeze again.
5 Add the remaining evaporated milk, condensed milk and sugar.
6 Bring to a gentle boil and remove from the heat.
7 Dissolve the gelatine in a little cold water. Add to the mixture and stir till cooled. Strain through a fine sieve into a mould and chill thoroughly,
8 To serve, turn out on a serving dish and decorate with coloured grated coconut. Make this by putting some grated coconut into a jar. Pour a few drops of the desired colouring over the coconut. Shake vigorously.
See illustration on page 101

'Let's go under de coconut tree, darlin',
Let's go under de coconut tree!'
(Traditional song)

JAMAICA RUM CUSTARD

175g (6oz) butter
juice of 2 limes
grated rind of 1 lime
110ml (4 fl oz) rum
275g (10oz) dark brown sugar
2 eggs

METHOD 1 Using a double boiler, place the ingredients into the top section.
2 With a rotary beater, beat the mixture over boiling water for about 5 minutes or until the sauce thickens.
3 Serve hot with puddings or try it on fruit cake! Scrumptious!

Note This sauce can be frozen for use later – adding more rum if you think this will help it!

JAMAICA TRIFLE
Serves 6-8

1 ginger cake
110ml (4 fl oz) rum
1 tin mangoes
575ml (1pt) custard
575ml (1pt) whipping cream
chocolate flakes for decoration

METHOD 1 Break the ginger cake into a glass bowl, covering the base with it.
2 Sprinkle the rum all over the cake.
3 Drain the syrup from the mangoes and, keeping a few pieces back for decoration, spread the rest over the cake.
4 Pour the made custard over the mangoes. Put the bowl into the refrigerator. Allow to cool and set.
5 Spread the fresh whipped cream over the set custard. Decorate with cream rosettes, mango pieces and chocolate flakes.

COLD RUM SOUFFLÉ
Serves 4

This is deliciously refreshing whether you use it as an after-dinner dessert, or as a summer lunchtime treat.

4 eggs
225ml (8fl oz) single cream
110g (4oz) caster sugar
2 sachets gelatine
a small amount of water to
    dissolve the gelatine
2 tsp vanilla essence
110ml (4 fl oz) dark rum
1 Kiwi fruit for decoration

METHOD 1 Separate the eggs. Whisk the fresh cream and put the bowl into the refrigerator to chill.
2 Whisk the egg yolks with the sugar until they are pale and fluffy.
3 Whisk the egg whites until they peak.
4 Dissolve the gelatine with the hot water. Allow to cool slightly.
5 In a large bowl, combine the yolks, whites and cream and fold in very carefully. Add the vanilla essence, dark rum and gelatine.
6 Pour into a deep soufflé dish and chill in the refrigerator for 30 minutes until set.
7 Decorate with slices of Kiwi fruit and rosettes of whipped cream.

Note You may use either sachet gelatine which will give you the directions for use, or 1 leaf of gelatine dissolved in about 2 tbsp of hot water.

BAKED LIME PUDDING
Serves 4

110g (4oz) caster sugar
3 eggs, separated
1 tsp cinnamon
225g (8oz) self-raising flour
2 limes, rind grated and juice
    strained
275ml ($\frac{1}{2}$pt) milk
4 tbsp rum

METHOD 1 Beat the sugar and the egg yolks together carefully.
2 Mix the cinnamon into the flour. Add to the mixture together with the grated rind and lime juice.
3 Gradually stir in the milk, then the rum.
4 Whisk the egg whites until they 'peak'. Fold into the mixture.
5 Pour into a buttered 20cm (8in) tin. Decorate the top with thin slices of lime and bake at 190°C (375°F) Reg 5 for 30-35 minutes in the centre of the oven.
See illustration on page 101

'One, one, full basket!'

FOOLISH PANCAKES
Serves 4

Where did this dish get its name?
I think it must be to do with the
filling. I mean, you've got to be
daft to want to put all that lot in a
pancake!

For the pancakes
110g (4oz) plain flour
2 tbsp sugar
2 eggs
275ml ($\frac{1}{2}$pt) milk
110ml (4 floz) oil for cooking

For the filling
1 medium mango
1 small pineapple
425ml ($\frac{3}{4}$pt) double cream
1 dsp sugar
5 tbsp coconut liqueur (e.g.
    Malibu) to taste
chocolate and nuts for garnish

METHOD 1 To make the
filling, peel the mango
and pineapple and slice.
2 Whip the cream until light and
fluffy.
3 Add fruit, sugar and coconut
liqueur to the cream.
4 To make the pancakes, sift flour
and mix in the sugar.
5 Make a well in the centre and
add the eggs. Add the milk slowly
and beat the mixture.
6 Add a little oil to the pancake
mix, stir in thoroughly and allow
to stand for about 15 minutes.
7 Lightly grease frying pan and
heat well.
8 Quickly pour the batter into the
pan until the base is thinly
covered.
9 Cook for 3–4 minutes, then turn
and cook the other side.
10 Spoon the filling into the
pancakes. Sprinkle with garnish
and serve.

FOOLISH RHUBARB

Serves 6-8

900g (2lb) rhubarb
110g (4oz) sugar
juice and rind of 2 large lemons
2-3 tbsp raspberry jam
1 sachet gelatine
175ml (6fl oz) double cream
$\frac{1}{4}$ tsp cochineal colouring
75g (3oz) softened, unsalted
    butter
fresh raspberries and blanched
    almonds for decoration

METHOD 1 Wash and cut the rhubarb into 2.5cm (1in) pieces.
2 In a pan, put the sugar, lemon juice and rind, jam and rhubarb. Cook until the rhubarb is a pulp. Push the mixture through a sieve.
3 Boil the gelatine, cream and cochineal colouring together. Remove from the heat and beat in the butter.
4 Stir the rhubarb 'pulp' in carefully.
5 Pour into individual glasses and decorate with the fresh raspberries and blanched almonds.

WIMBLEDON DELIGHT

Serves 2

In celebration of that unique British summer event, I wanted a change from the eternal and oh-so-ordinary Strawberries and Cream, so here is what I came up with…

2 punnets strawberries
2 dsp sugar
110ml (4 fl oz) orange liqueur
    (e.g. Grand Marnier)
1 l (1$\frac{3}{4}$pt) whipping cream
1 leaf of gelatine dissolved in a
    little hot water

METHOD 1 Mash down the strawberries with the sugar. (Keep a few whole strawberries back, and some cream for decoration.) Add the orange liqueur.
2 Whip the rest of the cream well, add to the strawberry mixture and fold in well.
3 Add the gelatine and gently fold in.
4 Put the mixture into a piping bag with a large star nozzle. Pipe into dishes, mounding the mixture.
5 Decorate with whipped cream and slices of the fruit.

MANGO HEDGEHOG
Serves 2

This is a novel sweet which I defy anyone to resist!

1 large mango
2 glacé cherries
1 strip angelica
fresh whipped cream or ice
      cream
chocolate vermicelli

METHOD 1 Cut the mango lengthways and separate the two halves. Remove the stone.
2 With a sharp knife, cut diagonally across each half-mango, forming a criss-cross pattern.
3 Turn each half inside out to make a spiky shape.
4 Place on a serving dish, add cherries for the eyes, a strip of angelica for the tail, pipe the fresh cream over and decorate with the chocolate vermicelli.

CORNMEAL PUDDING
Serves 6-8

575ml (1pt) milk
450g (1lb) sugar
225g (8oz) margarine
450g (1lb) fine cornmeal
110g (4oz) sultanas
1 tsp nutmeg
1 dsp vanilla essence
1 tsp salt
extra caster or icing sugar

METHOD 1 Dissolve the sugar and three-quarters of the margarine in the milk over a gentle heat.
2 Stir in the cornmeal, and cook on top of the stove, over a low heat until the mixture thickens (about 10 minutes).
3 Add the sultanas, nutmeg, vanilla and salt.
4. Pour the mixture into a greased tin, dot with the rest of the margarine and bake for $1\frac{1}{2}$ hours at 160°C (325°F) Reg 3. Leave to cool.
5. Sprinkle with caster or icing sugar and cut into wedges or squares when cold.

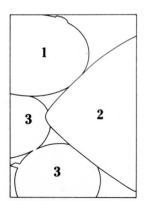

1 Rustie's Banana Fritters
2 Cornmeal Pudding 3 Mango Hedgehog

CAKES, BREADS AND BISCUITS

TIPSY CAKE

There are a few traditional English Tipsy Cakes, in which a sponge is usually soaked in sherry. Mrs Beeton has one which uses sherry or sweet wine plus 6 tablespoonfuls of brandy. I bet you didn't know she was such a raver! Anyway my version, would you believe, is generously drenched in rum, Tia Maria or Malibu.

1 large sponge cake or bought
    flan case
225ml (8fl oz) rum, Tia Maria or
    Malibu
575ml (1pt) whipped cream
110g (4oz) toasted almonds,
    flaked
glacé cherries, mangoes or
    strawberries

METHOD 1 Place the sponge cake or flan base on a large serving plate.
2 Sprinkle over the spirits. Allow to soak in.
3 Add the nuts to the whipped cream, saving some for decoration.
4 Spread the cream over the base or sponge cake. Decorate with the nuts and fruit according to taste.

BANANA CAKE

If you are looking for something different, both in taste and flavour, then try this. It is also an excellent way of using up those over-ripe bananas!

175g (6oz) butter
225g (8oz) caster sugar
2 eggs
5 large ripe bananas
450g (1lb) self-raising flour
2 tsp baking powder
chopped nuts (optional)

METHOD 1 Cream butter and sugar together until fluffy.
2 Add the eggs, one at a time, whisking continuously.
3 Keeping one back for garnishing, mash four bananas and beat into the mixture.
4 Sieve the flour and baking powder together and fold into the mixture. Add nuts, if liked.
5 Grease a loaf tin and put in the mixture. Slice the remaining banana and lay along the top of the cake mix.
6 Bake for 40 minutes at 180°C (350°F) Reg 4 or until firm.
7 Serve cold, sliced and spread with butter.

CARIBBEAN CRUNCH

675g (1½lb) granulated sugar
110ml (¼pt) water
110ml (4oz) butter
1 tbsp ground ginger
½ tbsp ground cinnamon
110g (4oz) crystallized ginger,
    chopped
110g (4oz) fresh coconut, finely
    grated

METHOD 1 Place the sugar,
water and butter into a
pan. Heat until the sugar is
dissolved.
2 Add the remaining ingredients
and bring to the boil.
3 When the mixture reaches the
'soft-ball' stage at around 120°C
(240°F), when a drop of the
mixture should form a ball when
dropped into cold water, remove
from the heat.
4 Beat until the mixture thickens.
5 Pour into a greased tin and
leave in the refrigerator until cold
and set. Cut into cubes.

RICEY RUM FINGERS

225g (8oz) white Patna rice,
    cooked
850ml (1½pt) milk
75g (3oz) brown sugar
2 tsp vanilla essence
3 egg yolks
4 tbsp rum

METHOD 1 Wash the rice and
cook in the milk with
40g (1½oz) sugar and the vanilla

essence for 20 minutes or until
tender.
2 Beat the egg yolks with the rum,
then beat into the rice mixture.
3 Spread the rice mixture into an
oblong shape, 1.2cm (½in) thick,
in a greased and floured flat tin.
4 Bake for 20–25 minutes at 200°C
(400°F) Reg 6.
5 Remove from the oven, cut into
fingers and dredge with icing
sugar.

RUM FUDGE

675g (1½lb) sugar
225ml (8fl oz) single fresh cream
200ml (7fl oz) sweetened
    condensed milk
1 pinch of cream of tartar
75g (3oz) chopped cherries
1 tsp vanilla essence
2 tsp rum

METHOD 1 Dissolve the sugar
in the fresh cream. Add
the condensed milk.
2 Over a low heat, cook gently
until the colour starts to change.
3 Add the cream of tartar (which
has been mixed with a little
water).
4 Beat with a wooden spoon, add
the chopped cherries, vanilla
essence and the rum. Beat again.
5 Pour the mixture into a 20cm
(8in) greased, flat tin. Spread
evenly over the base and allow to
set, cutting into squares before
the mixture sets.

Note This recipe *must* be
prepared quickly.

RUM BABAS

300g (11oz) plain flour
90g (3½oz) butter
¼ tsp salt
4 eggs
25g (1oz) yeast
25g (1oz) sugar

For the syrup
450g (1lb) sugar
850ml (1½pt) water
grated peel of 1 orange
grated peel of 1 lemon
85ml (3fl oz) rum

For the decoration
1×425g (15oz) tin fruit cocktail
110ml (4fl oz) fresh double
     cream

For the glaze
apricot jam

METHOD 1 Rub the fat and
       salt into the flour.
Break the eggs into a bowl, add
the yeast and sugar and beat with
the fingers or a spoon, until
'runny'.
2 Add the flour to this mixture
and make into a paste.
3 Well grease a savarin tin. Put
the mixture into a piping bag,
pipe into the tin and leave to rise,
for about 15 minutes.
4 Bake in a hot oven at 230°C
(450°F) Reg 8 for 20–25 minutes.
5 Remove from the oven and take
out of the tin. Leave to cool.
6 To make the syrup, boil the
sugar, water, orange and lemon
peel together for 15–20 minutes.
Leave to cool.
7 Sprinkle the cake with rum.
Soak the cake with the syrup and
glaze with the jam. Fill the centre
with the fruit or pile it around the
base. Complete with rosettes of
fresh, whipped cream.

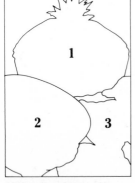

1 Pineapple and Mango Pie
2 Baked Lime Pudding 3 Rich
Coconut Pudding

RUM TRUFFLES

You know how children love to
get their hands into things that
are 'goo-ey'? Well, here is a recipe
that they can make themselves –
either as a special treat for tea or
as a present for someone special.
Encourage them to make a lovely
box to put the truffles in.

150ml (5fl oz) milk or plain
     chocolate
450g (1lb) well fruited cake
approx. 110ml (4fl oz) rum to
     bind
110g (4oz) vermicelli
1 packet sweet cases

METHOD 1 Put the chocolate
       pieces into a heat-
proof bowl over a pan of hot
water and heat gently until the
chocolate melts, stirring
occasionally.
2 Crumble the cake into a bowl,
and pour the rum over it, and
mould together.
3 Using your hands, roll small
balls of mixture. Dip into the
chocolate coating completely.
Roll into the vermicelli and place
into the paper cases.

CHOCOLATE RUM-BA GATEAU

Marvellous as a dessert for a very special dinner party or buffet, or just as a treat for yourself!

150g (5oz) butter
275g (10oz) soft brown sugar
4 eggs
350g (12oz) self-raising flour
1 tsp baking powder
1 tsp salt
65g (2½oz) cocoa powder
1 tsp vanilla essence
110ml (4fl oz) milk

For the rum syrup
175g (6oz) granulated sugar
150ml (¼pt) water
4 tbsp rum

For decoration
340 (12fl oz) double cream
chocolate flakes or curls

METHOD 1 Beat the butter and sugar until creamy.
2 Gradually add the eggs, one at a time, and beat in well.
3 Sieve the flour, baking powder, salt and cocoa powder together. Gently fold into the mixture.

4 Add the vanilla essence to the milk and fold into the mixture.
5 Pour into two 20cm (8in) greased and lined sponge tins. Bake at 180°C (350°F) Reg 4 for 35–40 minutes. Set aside to cool.
6 Make the syrup by putting the sugar and water into a saucepan. Stir over a low heat till the sugar dissolves, then bring to the boil. Take off the heat, allow to cool, and add the rum.
7 When the cake is cool, pour over the syrup and leave in the refrigerator for at least 2 hours.
8 To decorate, beat the fresh cream. Use half the double cream to sandwich the cake together. Use the other half to swirl rosettes of cream all over the top of the cake. Sprinkle with chocolate curls.

GIZADAS

These little coconut tartlets are known as 'Pinch-Me-Rounds' in Jamaica, and are very popular. They are delicious eaten as they are, or served with ice cream.

For the pastry
450g (1lb) plain flour
110g (4oz) margarine
50g (2oz) caster sugar
water to bind

For the filling
225g (8oz) desiccated coconut or fresh coconut, finely grated
110g (4oz) brown sugar
1-2 dsp caramel colouring
2 tsp nutmeg
2 tsp cinnamon
25g (1oz) margarine
2 tsp almond essence
2 tsp vanilla essence
170-225ml (6-8floz) water

METHOD 1 To make the pastry, rub the margarine and sugar into the flour, bind with the water and allow to stand for 10 minutes.
2 Roll out on a floured board and with a saucer cut 'rounds' from the pastry.
3 Pinch up each 'round' into a small pie-case. Place on a greased baking tray.
4 To make the filling, combine all the ingredients together and mix well.
5 Fill each pie-case with the mixture.
6 Bake at 180°C (350°F) Reg 4 for 20-25 minutes.
See illustration on page 105

COCONUT CAKE

Why not try using fresh coconut for this cake? The flavour is wonderful and the sultanas add a new dimension.

1 large fresh coconut or 450g (1lb) dessicated coconut.
225g (8oz) butter
225g (8oz) soft brown sugar
2 eggs
450g (1lb) self-raising flour
2 tsp baking powder
1 dsp vanilla essence
425ml ($\frac{3}{4}$pt) milk

METHOD 1 Grease and line a 25cm (10in) baking tin.
2 Crack coconut. Husk out the 'meat' and grate finely.
3 Cream butter, sugar and eggs (added gradually) for about 10 minutes.
4 To this batter, add flour, baking powder, grated or dessicated coconut and vanilla essence. Mix well together.
5 Add milk gradually until a 'runny' consistency is achieved. Stir in sultanas.
6 Pour into the greased and lined baking tin and bake at 160°C (325°F) Reg 3 for 2 hours. Turn out, cool and serve.

'Me darlin' Love, me lickle dove, Me dumplin, me gizada. Me Sweety Sue, I goes for you Like how flies goes for sugar.'
(From *Love Letta,* by Louise Bennett)

RUSTIE'S FRUITY JOURNEY CAKES

Great for using up windfall fruit from the garden. In the Caribbean they might be rose apples, mangoes or guavas, and to make this recipe you can either buy some of these or use your own domestic windfalls like apples and plums.

For the dough
900g (2lb) plain flour
50g (2oz) margarine
50g (2oz) sugar
2 tsp baking powder
water to bind

For the filling
450g (1lb) apples
450g (1lb) plums
110g (4oz) brown sugar
1 dsp mixed spice
25g (1oz) root ginger, peeled and
    chopped
175g (6oz) mixed fruit
110ml (4 fl oz) water
cornflour to thicken the mixture

METHOD 1 To make the dough, rub the margarine, baking powder and sugar into the flour. Bind together with the water to a dough.
2 Roll pieces of the dough into balls with the hands, then set aside.
3 On a floured board, roll out into 20cm (8in) rounds.
4 To make the filling, put the fruit, sugar and spices into a pan. Cook over a medium heat till pulped. Thicken the mixture with a little cornflour mixed with a little water.
5 Taking each round in turn, put a large spoonful of the filling into each. Fold over the dough and seal the edges with a fork.
6 Deep-fry the cakes for 5–8 minutes until golden brown. Serve with fresh cream and sprinkle with chocolate vermicelli.

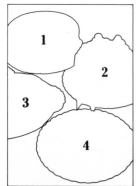

1 Rustie's Almond Beauty Cake
2 Rustie's Refrigerator Cake
3 Gizadas 4 Rustie's Fruity Journey Cakes

JOURNEY (OR JOHNNY) CAKES

These are so called because they were often taken by travellers to sustain them on long journeys, and are traditional Caribbean food. They are delicious, either on their own or with fish or meat.

450g (1lb) self-raising flour
1 tsp salt
1 tsp baking powder
50g (2oz) butter or margarine
150ml (¼pt) water
oil for deep frying

METHOD 1 Sieve the flour, salt and baking powder together. Rub in the margarine or butter.
2 Make into a dough with the water.
3 Roll small amounts of the mixture into little balls with the hands. Flatten the tops.
4 Heat the oil and deep-fry until golden brown (8–10 minutes). Alternatively, you can fry them in shallow oil for 4–5 minutes each side.

'De t'ing in de corner wid De freckles is me heart.'
(From *Love Letta*, by Louise Bennett)

FLAMING HEART

Specially created for St Valentine's Day, this cake will win any man's heart, so get busy with that 'old black magic' – you can't fail!

2×30cm (12in) sponge bases
1 large fresh pineapple
1 punnet strawberries
110ml (4floz) or more of rum!

For the meringue
150g (5oz) egg whites
560g (1¼lb) caster sugar

METHOD 1 Make the meringue mix by beating together the egg whites and sugar until the mixture is stiff and 'peaks'.
2 Cut the sponge bases into heart shapes.
3 Peel the pineapple and cut into rounds. Cut the strawberries in half. Place fruit on one sponge base and sprinkle with rum.
4 Cover with the other sponge base, using the cut-away sponge pieces to seal in the fruit.
5 Pipe meringue over the cake and decorate with the pieces of fruit left over.
6 Keep in freezer until ready for use. Before serving 'flash' in oven for 5–10 minutes.
7 For serving, fill an eggshell with rum and pour over the cake. Set the rum alight and serve with the lights turned down!

RUSTIE'S ALMOND BEAUTY CAKE

225g (8oz) butter or margarine
225g (8oz) caster sugar
4 (size 4) eggs, beaten
pinch of salt
450g (1lb) self-raising flour
275ml ($\frac{1}{2}$pt) milk
$\frac{1}{2}$ tsp pink colouring
75g (3oz) glacé cherries, washed
    and chopped
75g (3oz) chopped almonds

METHOD 1 Beat together the fat and sugar until pale and creamy. Gradually add the beaten eggs mixing in well. Add the salt to the flour and fold carefully into the mixture. Add the milk as required to give a soft dropping consistency.
2 Separate the mixture into two bowls – two-thirds in one and one-third in the other. To the larger amount add the pink colouring and the cherries. Add the almonds to the smaller quantity.
3 Divide the large amount between the two 20cm (8in) greased and base-lined sandwich tins. Put the remaining quantity into another prepared tin. Bake all three at 180°C (350°F) Reg 4 for 30 minutes.
4 Sandwich the cakes together with whipped double cream or butter cream. Dust the top with icing sugar before serving.
See illustration on page 105

RUSTIE'S REFRIGERATOR CAKE

275g (10oz) sugar
4 eggs
3 tsp instant coffee powder
3 tbsp cocoa powder
1 tsp rum essence
2 pkts Boudoir biscuits
575ml (1pt) whipping cream,
    whipped to a stiff peak
1 sachet or 2 leaves of gelatine
glacé cherries for decoration

METHOD 1 Whisk the eggs and sugar together, then add the eggs gradually.
2 Dissolve the coffee and cocoa powder in a little warm water. Add to the mixture with the rum essence. Whisk well.
3 Line a deep basin or cake tin with the sponge finger biscuits, covering the sides and bottom.
4 Add the whipped cream to the mixture and fold in with the gelatine.
5 Spoon the mixture into the centre of the container and fill to the top.
6 Fit a plate inside the top and weight it down. Chill the mixture in the refrigerator overnight. Remove the plate before serving.
7 To serve, ease round the sides of the cake with a palette knife. Place a serving plate over the top of the cake and turn upside down.
8 Decorate with rosettes of fresh cream and glacé cherries. Tie a red ribbon round the middle of the cake, and serve.
See illustration on page 105

CARIBBEAN CHRISTMAS CAKE

Jonkunnu is a procession of masked dancers who go through the streets wearing animal head masks and characters such as the Bride and the Devil. Having no money to pay for any Christmas treats, they take a collection from the watching crowd.

450g (1lb) sultanas
900g (2lb) mixed fruit
225g (8oz) stoned raisins
225g (8oz) currants
110g (4oz) chopped cherries
1 bottle ruby wine
450g (1lb) butter
450g (1lb) soft brown sugar
10 eggs
1 tbsp caramel colouring or
        treacle (according to taste)
450g (1lb) plain flour
110g (4oz) ground almonds
1 dsp cinnamon
1 dsp nutmeg
1 dsp vanilla essence
1 dsp rum flavouring
$\frac{1}{2}$ bottle rum

METHOD 1 Steam all fruit together in the ruby wine for about 15 minutes. Cool.
2 Cream butter and sugar together until fluffy then gradually add the eggs and caramel colouring.
3 Mix ground almonds with flour and add the cinnamon and nutmeg. Add dry ingredients to the creamed butter and fold in.
4 Mix all the fruit into the mixture adding vanilla essence and rum flavouring.
5 Place into a well-lined, greased tin and bake for 3 hours at 160°C (325°F) Reg 3.
6 Allow the cake to cool, then pour over $\frac{1}{2}$ bottle of rum, allowing it to soak in.
7 To keep the cake moist, wrap in foil until ready to decorate.

RUSTIE'S GINGER CAKE

175g (6oz) butter
110g (4oz) soft brown sugar
4 eggs beaten
110ml (4floz) golden syrup
225g (8oz) self-raising flour
1 tsp salt
25g (1oz) root ginger, peeled and
        grated or 2 tsp ground
        ginger
$\frac{1}{2}$ tsp cinnamon
1 tsp baking powder
28ml (1floz) milk

METHOD 1 Cream together the butter and sugar and add the eggs gradually.
2 Add the golden syrup, mixing in well.
3 Sieve together the flour, salt, spices and baking powder. Add to the mixture blending well.
4 Add the milk and mix to a 'dropping' consistency.
5 Pour into a well-greased loaf tin and bake at 180°C (350°F) Reg 4 for 35 minutes.

'Christmus a come, me wan' me lama' (presents)
(Traditional Jonkunnu song)

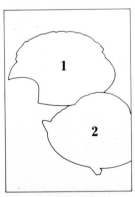

1 Caribbean Christmas Cake
2 Rustie's Christmas Pudding

Cakes, Breads and Biscuits

EASTER BUN

This is a traditional recipe, always eaten at Easter. The buns are served buttered with cheese.

1 egg
50g (2oz) yeast
175g (6oz) soft brown sugar
575ml (1pt) milk
275ml ($\frac{1}{2}$pt) water
1.4kg (3lb) strong bread flour
1 tsp salt
2 tsp caramel colouring
2 tsp nutmeg
2 tsp cinnamon
2 tsp mixed spice
50g (2oz) butter
450g (1lb) mixed fruit
110g (4oz) glacé cherries

For the bun wash
110g (4oz) soft brown sugar
275ml ($\frac{1}{2}$pt) water

METHOD 1 Break the egg into a bowl. Mash down the yeast, add the sugar and mix in with the fingers or a spoon. It will become runny.
2 Add the milk and water, half of the flour, the salt and the caramel colouring. Mix well and set aside for 30 minutes.
3 After this time, add the rest of the flour, the spices and the butter. Mix well and add the fruit.
4 Placing the mixture on a floured board, knead well for 5 minutes.
5 Shape into buns (large or small). Place on a greased baking sheet, sprinkle with a little warm water, and allow to rise for 12–15 minutes.
6 Bake in a hot oven at 220°C (425°F) Reg 7 for 35 minutes.

7 When cooked, glaze with the bun wash. Make this by putting the sugar and water into a saucepan and bringing to the boil, stirring all the time. Cook for 25–30 minutes, until boiled down. Brush this glaze over the buns to give them a smart finishing touch.

WEST INDIAN SPICE CAKE

450g (1lb) self-raising flour
1 tsp baking powder
$\frac{3}{4}$ tsp salt
$\frac{3}{4}$ tsp cinnamon
$\frac{1}{2}$ tsp cloves
225g (8oz) granulated sugar
225g (8oz) margarine
225g (8oz) brown sugar
2 eggs, beaten
275ml ($\frac{1}{2}$pt) buttermilk

METHOD 1 Make buttermilk by adding 2 tbsp vinegar to 275ml ($\frac{1}{2}$pt) milk.
2 Combine all the ingredients in a mixing bowl.
3 Beat for 2 minutes with a rotary mixer at low speed until fully blended.
4 Grease and line two 23cm (9in) sponge tins. Pour in the batter and spread level.
5 Bake at 190°C (375°F) Reg 5 for 25–35 minutes.

RUSTIE'S GINGER BICKIES

250g (9oz) butter
225g (8oz) sugar
50g (2oz) root ginger, peeled and
　　　grated
1 tsp cinnamon
pinch of salt
2 tbsp cocoa
250g (9oz) plain flour
50g (2oz) root ginger, peeled and
　　　sliced for decoration

METHOD 1 Cream the butter
and the sugar. Add the
ginger, cinnamon, salt and cocoa
to the flour.
2 Combine both mixtures and
blend well.
3 Roll out on a floured
board to 3mm ($\frac{1}{8}$in) thickness.
4 Cut into small rounds with
a biscuit cutter.
5 Place 2 strips of sliced root
ginger on the top of each round
and place on a greased baking
sheet.
6 Bake at 180°C (350°F) Reg 4 for
8–10 minutes until golden brown.

RUSTIE'S NUTTY CREAM FREEZE

275ml ($\frac{1}{2}$pt) milk
20 marshmallows
2 tsp rum essence
425ml ($\frac{3}{4}$pt) double cream,
    whipped
175g (6oz) chopped nuts

METHOD 1 Dissolve the marshmallows and milk together over a low heat. Add the rum essence.
2 Remove from the heat and allow to cool.
3 Fold in the whipped cream and nuts.
4 Spread the mixture out in a flat tray and freeze.
5 When half frozen, cut into squares.

RUSTIE'S LITTLE TREATS

Here is an unusual recipe for when you are looking for something other than peanuts or crisps to accompany drinks:

1 coconut
salt and sugar

METHOD 1 Break open the coconut and remove the 'meat'.
2 Slice very thinly and lay out on a baking sheet. Brown under a grill.
3 Sprinkle half of the 'crisps' with sugar and the other half with salt.
4 Serve from dishes with your drinks.

COCO BREAD

40g (1$\frac{1}{2}$oz) yeast
2 tsp sugar
575ml (1pt) milk, warmed
1 tsp salt
1.4kg (3lb) strong bread flour
175g (6oz) butter

METHOD 1 Dissolve the yeast with the sugar in a bowl and add the milk.
2 Mix the salt with the flour. Rub in 50g (2oz) of the butter.
3 Add this mixture to the liquid, stir together and mix well. Knead and allow to stand for 15–20 minutes.
4 Press the dough down firmly and knead again for 5–6 minutes.
5 Cut into 225g (8oz) pieces and shape each into a ball. Then, with a rolling pin, roll out to 'rounds' about 20cm (8in) in diameter.
6 Dot the top all over with butter. Fold in half. Dot with butter again and fold over.
7 Using a clean finger, press 'hollows' into the top, and place the bread on a baking tray. Allow to rise again until doubled in size.
8 Sprinkle with water and bake in a hot oven at 220°C (425°F) Reg 7 for 30–35 minutes.

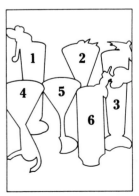

1 Ginger Beer **2** Mango Wizz
3 Rustie's Aphrodisiac **4** Frozen Daiquiri **5** Rustie's Black Cow
6 Classic Planter's Punch

PUMPKIN BREAD

This is a really moist, rich loaf, with a delectable taste. And it's so easy to make!

450g (1lb) self-raising flour
1 tsp cinnamon
1 tsp nutmeg
1 tsp salt
225g (8oz) granulated sugar
175g (6oz) margarine
2 eggs
275g (10oz) pumpkin, cooked
    and mashed
175g (6oz) seedless raisins

METHOD 1 Sieve together the flour, cinnamon, nutmeg and salt.
2 Beat the sugar and margarine for about 10 minutes.
3 Add the eggs gradually, beating until creamy.
4 Gently fold in the flour mixture then the mashed pumpkin. Add the raisins and stir well.
5 Bake in a lined, greased loaf tin at 180°C (350°F) Reg 4 for 1 hour. Serve spread with butter.

DUCK BREAD

This bread is made with what is called a 'tight' dough. It is traditional in the Caribbean, and is used at Christmas or at a wedding. Shaped like a duck, you make two, which are placed either side of the Festive cake.

1 dsp salt
1.4kg (3lb) strong bread flour
75g (3oz) cooking fat, e.g.
    Whitecap
40g (1½oz) fresh yeast
575ml (1pt) water

METHOD 1 Sift the salt and flour together and rub in the fat.
2 Dissolve the yeast in warm (bloodheat) water.
3 Gradually bind the dry ingredients together with the liquid.
4 Mould the dough continually by hand for about 10 minutes, on a well-floured board.
5 Return the dough to the bowl, cover with a damp cloth or piece of polythene and leave in a warm place to rise until doubled in size.
6 Halve the dough and roll into separate balls. Roll out into individual oblong pieces, approx. 30×30cm (12×12in).
7 Roll each into a Swiss-roll shape. From each, cut off ⅓ (to make the head).
8 Mould the 'body' into a duck shape. Damp head end with water. Mould head, and stick both together. Using a knife, fork or scissors, decorate with 'feathers'.
9 Sprinkle with warm water, place on a greased tray, and allow to rise for 10-15 minutes in a warm place.
10 Heat the oven to 230°C (450°F) Reg 8. Place a meat tin containing a small amount of water at the bottom of the oven to cause steam, and bake the 'ducks' in the centre of the oven for 40-45 minutes.

GROTTO
Makes 3

No-one quite knows how this bread got its name it probably comes from the word 'gâteau', but even that isn't clear! It is a soft milk bread, rather like Coco Bread, and can be eaten hot or cold with meats or cheese. Or the dough can be made into plaits and used for a wedding breakfast.

50g (2oz) fresh yeast
1 tbsp caster sugar
575ml (1pt) milk
1.4kg (3lb) strong bread flour
1 dsp salt
200g (7oz) margarine

METHOD 1 Well grease a baking tray.
2 Dissolve the yeast and sugar in a bowl using the fingers.
3 Pour on the milk, warmed to bloodheat, and whisk together.
4 Sift the flour and salt into a bowl and run in the fat.
5 Whisk half the flour mixture into the yeast/milk mixture. Stand for 30 minutes.
6 Add the remaining flour mixture to the fermenting yeast/milk mixture and make into a dough.
7 Turn out on a well-floured board and mould for about 10 minutes,until the dough becomes 'elastic-ky'. (If the dough is sticky, add a little more flour.)

8 Cut the dough into 3 equal pieces. Mould into 'rounds', and allow to stand in a warm place until doubled in size.
9 Roll out on a well-floured board into approx. 20cm (8in) rounds, 2.5cm (1in) thick.
10 Brush with water, fold in half and then into quarters.
11 Prick all over with a fork. Place on the baking tray. Allow to rise in a warm place for 45 minutes.
12 Sprinkle with warm water and bake in a hot oven at 220°C (425°F) Reg 7 for 50 minutes.

DRINKS

You cannot go far in the Caribbean without meeting our national drink – rum. A seventeenth century traveller in Barbados described it as 'Rumbullion of Kill-Devill, distilled from sugar canes, a hot, hellish and terrible liquor.'

Its name may come from the Spanish word 'ron' or from the old Devonshire word for strong drink, 'rumbustion'. Sailors fighting against gales round the Islands would often speak of 'comfort waters' and in old books there are stories involving 'Barbados waters'. It became popular in England in the eighteenth century, and in the Caribbean it was given to the slaves to ease their misery and to bring a sort of contentment to their miserable lives.

'Darg hab liberty watch gubnor.'

Rum is almost magical, in that it cools 'when the spirits are exhausted with much sweating', as someone put it, and yet it warms when winter chills strike.

In those far-off slaving days, rum was a sweet, heavy and pungent drink. Today's rums vary from dark and luscious to white and light, but they are all Hmmmmmmmmm!

In the Caribbean it is so hot that everyone naturally goes in for a lot of fruits and juices which they liquidize together and mix with alcohol – usually rum. They have a marvellous choice of fruits to work with, and the colours also give an extra lift to the cocktail-type drinks which are so popular. It is not surprising, then, that most of the drinks in this section are basically of the cocktail family. A few years ago, some of them might have seemed really strange, but things are different now that cocktails have caught on much more in Britain.

When you prepare one of these drinks, by the way, don't forget the decorations. Put a flower on top of the liquor, and lay in plenty of brightly coloured straws and bar mats.

Small Public Health Warning! If you are not quite used to the 'pace' of cocktail drinking, the important thing to remember is that each drink contains a pretty stiff slug of booze. Sometimes people are taken in by the lovely colours, the cream and the crushed ice, and go knocking back their cocktails like they were some kind of de-luxe fruit juice. Later their head lifts off and they wonder why! Anyway, I just thought I'd mention it. Cheers!

CLASSIC PLANTER'S PUNCH
Serves 2

170ml (6fl oz) dark rum
57ml (2fl oz) lime cordial or lime
    juice and 3 tbsp caster sugar
dash Angostura bitters
185ml ($\frac{1}{3}$pt) crushed ice

METHOD 1 Shake all the
ingredients together.
2 Divide between 2 chilled
tumblers.
3 Rest a long spoon on the
surface of each drink and
carefully pour 1 tbsp rum down
the stem so that it stays on the
surface.
4 Sprinkle with grated nutmeg
and decorate with sliced fruit.
See illustration on page 112

FROZEN DAIQUIRI
Serves 2

170ml (6fl oz) light rum
28ml (1fl oz) lime cordial
425ml ($\frac{3}{4}$pt) ice

METHOD 1 Liquidize all
ingredients for 20
seconds.
2 Turn straight into chilled
glasses and serve.
See illustration on page 112

RUSTIE'S PUNCH
Serves 4

A very simple recipe to follow and
guaranteed to get the party going!

1×425ml ($\frac{3}{4}$pt) can condensed milk
150g (5oz) sugar
575ml (1pt) water
$\frac{1}{2}$×425ml ($\frac{3}{4}$pt) evaporated milk
1×275ml ($\frac{1}{2}$pt) can Guinness
2 tsp vanilla essence
2 tsp almond essence
1 tsp nutmeg
$\frac{1}{4}$ bottle Jamaican rum
ice cubes, mashed up

METHOD 1 Add the
condensed milk and
sugar to the pint of water and
whisk until sugar completely
dissolved.
2 Add all the other ingredients,
stir and serve.

RUSTIE'S BANANA SHAKE
Serves 1

Just the thing for a really hot day!

275ml ($\frac{1}{2}$pt) milk
1 large banana, not too ripe,
    peeled and roughly
    chopped
2 tbsp natural yogurt
1 tbsp clear honey
pinch of nutmeg

METHOD 1 Put all the
ingredients into a
blender. Liquidize until smooth.
2 If the consistency is too thick,
just add a little more milk.
3 Taste, and if too sweet, stir in a
little lemon juice. Serve in a
chilled glass.

BUTTERY RUM TODDY
Serves 1

There's nothing better than this toddy to warm you up and to keep colds and chills at bay!

2 tsp cinnamon or 1 cinnamon
  stick
110ml (4fl oz) light rum
knob of unsalted butter
275ml ($\frac{1}{2}$pt) boiling cider
pinch of nutmeg

METHOD 1 Put the cinnamon
into a jug.
2 Add the rum and butter. Pour on the boiling cider.
3 Stir well until the butter is dissolved. Sprinkle with nutmeg.

'When puss gone, ratta take house.'

PAW-PAW AND PINEAPPLE KICK
Serves 6

1 medium paw-paw
1 medium pineapple
110g (4oz) white or soft brown
  sugar
575ml (1pt) pineapple juice
1×225g (8oz) can sweetened
  condensed milk
275ml (8fl oz) dark rum

METHOD 1 Peel the
paw-paw,
remove the seeds
and chop.
2 Cut the pineapple into small pieces.
3 Blend all ingredients for 2 minutes. Serve with ice.

RUSTIE'S BLACK COW
Serves 1

This is a favourite cocktail at my restaurant!

METHOD 1 Mix equal
quantities of Tia Maria
and double cream.
2 Pour into a glass filled with crushed ice.
3 Sprinkle with chocolate curls. Yummy!
See illustration on page 112

COCONUT PINEAPPLE EXOTICA
Serves 4-5

1 large fresh coconut, grated
725ml (1$\frac{1}{4}$pt) cold water
1 small pineapple, peeled and
  chopped
2 tbsp caster sugar
225ml (8fl oz) light rum

METHOD 1 Liquidize the
coconut with 575ml
(1pt) water at high speed.
2 Strain to extract the juice.
3 Liquidize the pineapple and caster sugar with the remaining 150ml ($\frac{1}{4}$pt) water.
4 Strain through a sieve to extract the juice.
5 In a jug, combine the juices with the rum. Chill.
6 Serve with crushed ice.

RUSTIE'S APHRODISIAC
Serves 4-6

West Indians are great believers in aphrodisiac drinks, such as Strongback. I remember my mother making this type of drink for us and my father, so, if you think you need it–here's my recipe.

1 large paw-paw
1 large mango
1 large ripe banana
110g (4oz) sugar
$\frac{1}{2}$ small tin condensed milk
275ml ($\frac{1}{2}$pt) water
3 ice cubes
340ml (12floz) dark rum
$\frac{1}{2}$ tsp ground nutmeg

METHOD 1 Peel the paw-paw and remove the seeds. Cut fruit into large segments.
2 Peel the mango, cut the flesh from the large seed in the centre and dice into small pieces.
3 Peel and dice the banana.
4 Place the fruit in a liquidizer with the sugar and milk. Beat until smooth.
5 Add the water and ice cubes and, finally, the rum. Beat again until very smooth, then serve in chilled glasses. Sprinkle with nutmeg.
See illustration on page 112

KNOCKOUT ORANGE
Serves 10

If you have a big party in the offing, then make this drink and keep it. It improves greatly with age!

14 oranges (try to include at least 2 Seville oranges)
900g (2lb) granulated sugar
1.1l (2pt) rum

METHOD 1 Wash and thinly peel the oranges.
2 Squeeze the juice and strain to remove the pips.
3 Dissolve the sugar in the orange juice over a low heat, together with the peel. *Do not boil.*
4 Pour into an earthenware jug or container with a lid, and cover; when cool, add the rum and stir well.
5 Leave for about 3 weeks.
6 When ready to serve, remove the peel. Serve with crushed ice.

4 O'CLOCK PUNCH
Serves 6

1.1l (2pt) fresh boiling water
4-6 tsp tea
110g (4oz) soft brown sugar
150ml ($\frac{1}{4}$pt) lemon juice.
275ml ($\frac{1}{2}$pt) orange juice.
575ml (1pt) ginger ale
2 sprigs mint and orange slices for decoration

METHOD 1 In a large pot or container, pour in the boiling water. Add the tea and sugar. Stir and allow to brew. Strain and cool.
2 Combine the juices and ginger ale. Stir well and add to the tea.
3 Serve with crushed ice and decorate with orange slices and mint leaves.

MANGO WIZZ
Serves 1

1 large mango
1 tsp vanilla essence
1 dsp coconut or banana liqueur
1 dsp caster sugar
225ml (8fl oz) whipping cream

METHOD 1 Peel the mango and cut all the flesh away from the stone.
2 Place all the ingredients into a liquidizer and beat until smooth.
3 Whisk in the cream.
4 Pour into glass goblets, pipe a blob of cream on the top. Garnish with a slice of mango and chocolate vermicelli.
5 Chill until ready to serve.

Paw-paw or pineapple can be used as alternatives, but whatever you choose the taste is heavenly!
See illustration on page 112

'Me brudda did a tell me da You go Mango Walk.'
(Traditional song)

COCONUT HEAVEN
Serves 4

110g (4oz) coconut, cut from the shell and chopped
110g (4oz) white sugar
1×225g (8oz) can sweetened condensed milk
575ml (1pt) lemonade
225ml (8fl oz) coconut liqueur, e.g. Malibu

METHOD 1 Put the coconut, white sugar, condensed milk and lemonade into a blender.
2 Liquidize together for 2 minutes, then strain through a fine sieve and add the coconut liqueur.
3 Serve with ice.

RUSTIE'S EGG-NOG
Serves 6

4×425ml (¾pt) cans sweetened condensed milk
50g (2oz) caster sugar
6 medium eggs
grated peel and juice of 1 lemon or lime
2 tsp vanilla essence
575ml (1pt) rum (or more, according to taste!)
1 dsp nutmeg

METHOD 1 Whisk the condensed milk, sugar and eggs together.
2 Add the lemon or lime and vanilla essence.
3 Finally, add the rum and mix in well.
4 Pour into glasses, sprinkle with nutmeg and serve with crushed ice.

GINGER BEER
Serves 8

1 root ginger, grated, or 225g (8oz) ground ginger
1 tsp cinnamon
450g (1lb) white granulated sugar
1 lemon
2.8l (5pt) water

METHOD 1 Grate root ginger into saucepan.
2 Add cinnamon, sugar and lemon zest.
3 Boil in 2.2l (4pt) water for 10 minutes.
4 Strain into jug. Add remaining 575ml (1pt) cold water, and allow to chill in refrigerator.
5 Serve with crushed ice. Float lemon slices on top.

Note For Mums and Dads – it's great with rum!
See illustration on page 112

MANGO FLIP
Serves 3-4

2 large mangoes, peeled and
    chopped
175g (6oz) white sugar
110g (4oz) sweetened
    condensed milk
225ml (8fl oz) rum
575ml (1pt) orange juice

 1 Peel the mangoes,
    halve and discard the
stones.
2 Blend the remaining flesh with
the other ingredients for 2
minutes.
3 Serve with ice.

COOL WATERMELON
Serves 4-6

$\frac{1}{2}$ large watermelon
110g (4oz) white sugar
170ml (6fl oz) strawberry cordial
225ml (8fl oz) vodka

METHOD 1 Chop
    the flesh of
the melon and
liquidize with the other
ingredients for 2
minutes.
2 Strain through a fine
sieve and serve with ice.

INDEX

Page numbers in italics refer to illustrations

If you want to sample Rustie's Caribbean food here is the address of her restaurant;

Rustie's Caribbean Restaurant
192 Soho Hill
Hockley
Birmingham B19 1AP.

However, if you would like to write to Rustie about cookery or any other of her activities the address is;

Rustie's Club
PO Box 289
Hockley
Birmingham B19 1AR.